DESTINATION

WEST

Produced by the
Publications Division of the Automobile Association
Fanum House,
Basingstoke, Hampshire RG21 2EA

Produced by the Publications Division of the
Automobile Association
Researched and written by **Roland Weisz**
Editor **Richard Powell**
Art Editors **Keith Russell** and **M A Preedy**
Picture Research **Sally Howard**
Editorial Contributors **Barry Francis, Gail
Harada, Roger Prebble** and **Pat Rowlinson**
Editorial Adviser **Professor Esmond Wright,**
Director of the Institute of United States Studies,
University of London
Maps produced by the Cartographic Department of
the Automobile Association. Based on cartography
supplied by the American Automobile Association.
All maps © 1981 The American Automobile
Association

ISBN 0 86145 107 4

The Publishers would like to acknowledge the
extremely valuable help given to them in the
preparation of this book by the American Automobile
Association (AAA), 8111 Gatehouse Road, Falls
Church, Virginia 22047.
The AAA has prepared all the town plans and route
maps. They have also devised the routes followed by
the motor tours and the route information has been
checked by AAA road reporters, who make an annual
survey of all US roads. The names, addresses and
telephone numbers of museums, places of interest
and public buildings are in general based on the
information supplied by the AAA and every effort
has been made to ensure that it is accurate. The
publishers are also grateful to the following for
providing facilities and help during the preparation of
material for this book: Pan American World Airways
Inc; the Hertz Corporation; Hyatt Regency Hotels;
The United States Travel and Tourism
Administration
Professor Esmond Wright, Director of the Institute
of United States Studies, the University of London,
has provided valuable help in the reading of the
manuscript.

Filmset in Monophoto Plantin by
Servis Filmsetting Ltd, Manchester
Litho reproduction by
Mullis · Morgan Ltd, London

Printed and bound by Graficromo, S. A., Cordoba

Published by the Automobile Association,
Fanum House, Basingstoke, Hampshire RG21 2EA

The Publishers would like to thank the following
organisations, photographers and picture libraries for
the use of photographs in this book:
BIOFOTOS; J Allan Cash Ltd; Bruce Coleman;
Elisabeth Photo Library; Historic New Orleans
Collection; KOS; Mansell Collection; Photographers'
Library; PICTUREPOINT; SPECTRUM; Richard
Surman; United States Travel Service; ZEFA

Contents

Cover photographs:

U *The lights of Las Vegas, Nevada*
S *One of the famous San Francisco cable cars, California*
A *A traditional jazz player in New Orleans, Louisiana*

Title page photographs:

U *A streetcar in New Orleans, Louisiana*
S *Golden Gate Bridge, San Francisco*
A *Mission San Carlos Borromeo, Carmel, California*

Introduction

As a practical, on the spot guide, this book will delight the first-time traveller to the United States. It is packed with fact and practical information – where to stay, where to eat, and what to see. For those who have crossed the Atlantic before, these pages can serve as a happy reminder of past trips, or assist and suggest further exploration of this exciting continent. Others, who prefer to travel from the comfort of their own armchairs, will find the photographs and text make a valuable addition to the fireside library. This book helps you to enjoy the best the USA has to offer.

Destination USA West deals specifically with those states around the great cities of New Orleans, Los Angeles, Las Vegas and San Francisco. A sister volume concentrates on the cities and states of the Atlantic coast. Each of the four areas described here is divided into three sections. Firstly, the states and cities are introduced; secondly, detailed motor tours are given, accompanied by clearly marked maps; the final section is devoted to the major city of the area. Throughout, information on what to see, where to stay and where to eat is listed alongside places described in the book.

The Bayou State – *A paddle steamer, Louisiana*

The Golden West – *Pacific Palisades, S California*

Grand Canyon Country – *Grand Canyon, Arizona*

The Redwood Empire – *Yosemite Park, N California*

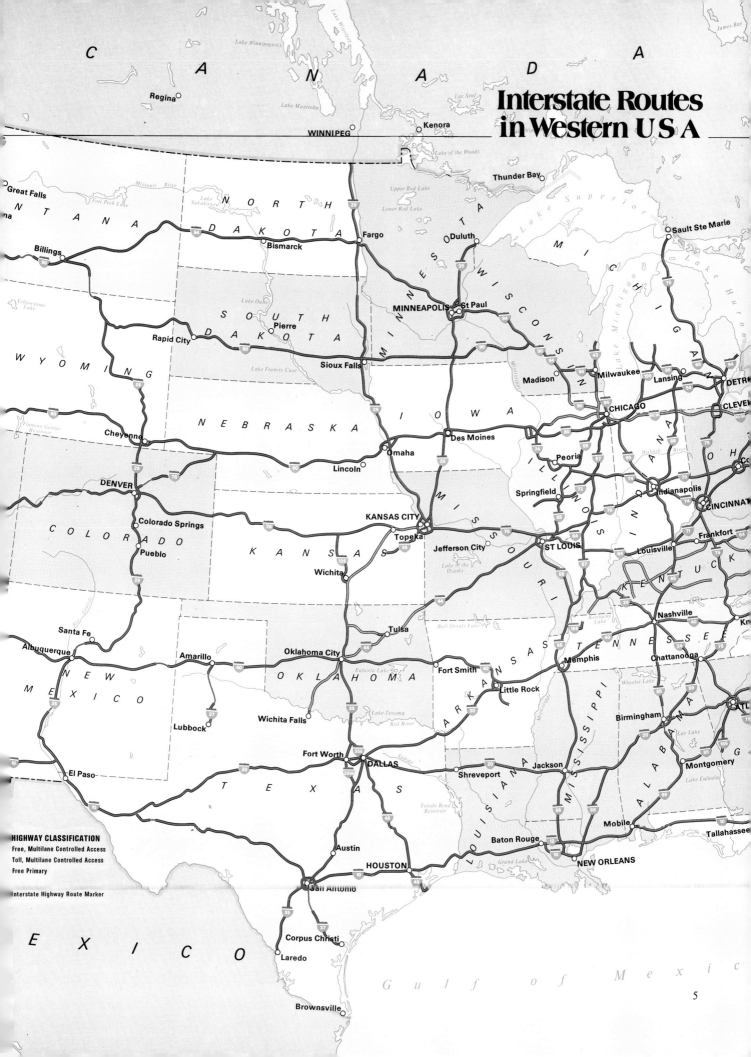

Interstate Routes
in Western USA

HIGHWAY CLASSIFICATION
Free, Multilane Controlled Access
Toll, Multilane Controlled Access
Free Primary

Interstate Highway Route Marker

5

Useful Information

Although the British and Americans may speak the same language, remember that America is a foreign country, with attitudes and customs often radically different to those we are used to in Europe. To help the tourist adjust a little more smoothly to the American lifestyle we have listed here some of the things you need to know for a visit to the United States.

ENTRY REGULATIONS

To enter the United States you require two essential documents; a visa, and a full British passport, which must be valid for at least six months after your intended return home. NB – the one-year British Visitors' Passport is not valid for the USA. Most travel agents carry application forms for visas, and may undertake to obtain the visa on your behalf. Otherwise, apply to the American Embassy, Visa Branch, 5 Upper Grosvenor Street, London W1A 2JB, tel 01 499 3443 (recorded information), and enclose a stamped addressed envelope, your passport, and evidence of your intention to leave the USA after your holiday (such as your return ticket or a letter from your employer stating that you will be returning to work). Normally you should allow at least four weeks for your application to be completed, but in an emergency you can apply personally to the Visa Branch (open 8am to 3pm, Monday to Friday, except for public holidays, 25 May and 3 July), but you may have to queue for anything up to three hours. Visas may also be obtained from the American Consulates in Edinburgh and Belfast. The addresses are: American Consulate General, 3 Regent Terrace, Edinburgh EH7 5BW; American Consulate General, Queen House, 14 Queen Street, Belfast BT1 6EQ.

CUSTOMS REGULATIONS

When you reach the USA, you will have to pass through immigration. This is usually a formality, but immigration officials will want to know where you intend to stay. You are allowed to bring the following duty-free items into the USA: one US quart of spirits or wine (persons ages 21 or over, although local state laws may vary); 200 cigarettes, or 50 cigars, or 3lbs of tobacco, or proportionate amounts of each; $100 worth of gifts, provided you are staying more than 72 hours and have not visited in the previous six months. You may bring $5,000 in personal funds into the USA.

CURRENCY

The basic unit of American currency is the dollar bill ($1.00 = 100 cents). Paper notes come in $1, $2, $5, $10, $20, $50, $100, $500 and $1,000 denominations, all of which are printed in the same colour and are the same size. Coins are minted in denominations of 1c (penny), 5c (nickel), 10c (dime), 25c (quarter), 50c and $1. You can exchange your own currency into US dollars at most major American banks. It is always best to change your currency at airports or in the larger cities, where you will receive a better exchange rate. Normal banking hours are 9am to 3pm, Monday to Friday. Credit cards such as American Express, Access (American Master Card), Barclaycard/VISA and Diners Club are accepted almost everywhere, and travellers cheques, either in sterling or dollars, are usually accepted by banks, hotels, restaurants or shops.

TRAVEL

AIR: More than 600 cities are covered by the internal flight network, and it is the best way to travel large distances. Foreign travellers can claim special discount fares on many airlines. A Visit USA Fare (VUSA) worth a 40% discount is one example, and there are several go-as-you-please packages. Ask your travel agent for details.

RAIL: Inter-city trains are generally cheaper than going by air over shorter distances. AMTRAK is the major passenger railway network, and their agents in Britain are Thomas Cook (England and Wales) and Thistle Air (Scotland). Your travel agent will be able to make arrangements for you.

BUSES: Luxurious coaches provide the most economical method of long distance travel. Greyhound and Trailways are the largest bus companies, and together with their smaller counterparts cover 120,000 miles of America's excellent highways. Passes entitling you to unlimited, nationwide travel can be bought in advance in the UK through your travel agent.

MOTORING: Major roads in America are well-surfaced, wide, and well signposted. Americans tend to think in terms of how long a journey may take, although distances are calculated in miles. Local roads are not so well surfaced and are often narrow. Controlled access highways are variously known as interstates, expressways or toll roads. Roads designated US, followed by a number, are similar to British main trunk roads. Interstate roads are equivalent to motorways. State Routes are main roads within a state, and Local Routes are minor roads. Toll roads and turnpikes charge a toll of 2–3 cents per mile and as access is limited on these super-highways, you should plan your exit points and rest stops well in advance. Often you will find that the cashier at petrol stations (gas stations) sits behind a bullet-proof kiosk, and may insist that you pay before filling up. When buying petrol, remember that American pints, quarts and gallons are smaller than the Imperial equivalents by about one-fifth, therefore a US gallon is about four-fifths of a British one. Hire cars usually use only lead-free petrol, a more expensive grade. There will be a notice in the car stating whether it uses this grade or not.

CAR HIRE: Hire cars are available at airports, car hire agencies, and rental offices in hotels. Local AAA clubs will recommend reputable agencies. There is usually a wide choice of vehicles, which you are able to inspect before you hire. Campers – motorised caravans – are readily available and come with all mod cons, but it is best to reserve one to avoid disappointment. The American Automobile Association can supply a list of approved camping sites to members of the British AA. Their address is the American Automobile Association (AAA), 8111 Gatehouse Road, Falls Church, Virginia 22047. Some car hire companies will rent to drivers of 18 years of age, others require you to be over 21, and in some areas drivers must be over 25. The major credit cards are universally acceptable, and travellers' cheques are taken. You will be asked to produce your passport and driving licence as proof of identification. Prices vary from one region to another, and include oil, maintenance and liability insurances. State and local taxes are additional, and petrol is usually extra. Most American cars have automatic transmission, and are often air-conditioned, a necessity in some regions where the summers can be very hot.

DRIVING REGULATIONS

Rules and hints are listed here which will help you to drive safely in America. Driving in the USA is not difficult, but it is helpful, and polite, to forearm yourself with knowledge of those general practices Americans take for granted. Each state has its own traffic regulations, however, so this list is only general. Local AAA offices will give advice about local regulations

1 Drive on the right of the road.
2 Keep to the speed limits; 20–25 miles per hour in cities and congested areas, 55 miles per hour on open roads.
3 Report any accident to the nearest police department immediately.
4 Strictly observe all traffic lights and stop, slow and caution signs. Normally, however, cars can filter right on red, provided they have first halted and checked that the road is clear. This does not apply in New York.
5 Do not pass on bends, at junctions or near the top of hills.
6 Do not pass school buses which have stopped to allow children to get on or off. This applies both when you are following the bus and when you are approaching it.
7 Observe reduced speed limits in all school zones.

8 Do not park on the highway in rural areas. If you must stop, pull right off the road.
9 Observe parking zone laws in cities, or your car may be towed away. Always park facing the flow of traffic and never double-park. Kerbside colour codes are: red for no parking; yellow for unloading commercial vehicles; white for unloading passengers; blue for parking for handicapped people; green for short-term (this often means literally 12 minutes). These may vary from state to state.
10 Always signal when you turn, stop or change lanes. Remember, however, that on many multi-lane highways Americans may overtake you on both sides, and may themselves change lane without signalling.

Watch your positioning on near-side lanes of highways. These sometimes become exit lanes only, and you may not see the sign saying 'Right Lane Must Exit' until too late. Many stretches of roadway on fast highways are heavily studded. This is an effective deterrent to speeding, as the noise of the drumming of the tyres is most alarming. On urban highways, keep an eye on the speed limits. You can move within moments from a 40 mph zone to a 45 mph zone, and back down to a 30 mph zone.
11 Cars carrying fewer than four people may be barred from certain privileged lanes of highways, especially at rush hours. These express lanes by-pass hold-ups at junctions, and are designed to encourage car-sharing.
12 Keep a lookout for cyclists – they are allowed to ride towards oncoming traffic.
13 Always lock your car when it is unattended.
14 Never pick up hitch-hikers.
15 Never call a sidewalk a pavement. To an American, the pavement is the roadway, and using the English term could lead to confusion if you have to have dealings with the police.

MEDICAL TREATMENT

The charges for medical treatment are high in the USA, so it is essential that you insure yourself before you leave. If you need a doctor or dentist, your hotel will contact one for you. Alternatively your embassy or consulate will supply a list of approved doctors.

HOTELS AND RESTAURANTS

It is worth taking a little time in selecting your hotel, and advisable to make reservations. Breakfast is seldom included in the price of a room. Remember many hotels in the cities offer cheap weekend rates to keep the rooms filled. Restaurants are not over expensive by British standards, and American food at its best is excellent. Portions are often larger than you are probably used to, and salad is frequently served without question as a first course. It is common to wait for a 'hostess' to show you to your table, and send someone to take your order. Tipping is expected – $12\frac{1}{2}\%$ or 15% is normal. Sometimes restaurants serve meals or bar drinks more cheaply during a 'happy hour', between 4 and 7pm.

PUBLIC HOLIDAYS

There are a number of public holidays celebrated in America which may be unfamiliar to the tourist. The principle ones are:

Washington's Birthday	Third Monday in February
Memorial Day	Last Monday in May
Independence Day	4 July
Labor Day	First Monday in September
Columbus Day	Second Monday in October
Veterans' Day	11 November
Thanksgiving Day	Fourth Thursday in November

Lincoln's Birthday, Armistice Day and Yom Kippur are designated public holidays in certain states or areas.

TOURIST INFORMATION

There are State Tourist Departments in every state, whose staff will help you with advice and information on every aspect of your holiday. They will also supply literature and maps to help you get the best out of your visit. Addresses of these departments may be obtained from the United States Travel Services, US Department of Commerce, 22 Sackville Street, London W1.

TELEPHONES

Public telephones are plentiful in the USA, and are found in restaurants, garages, hotel foyers, tobacconists, railway stations, airports and in telephone boxes on the pavements. Local calls cost from 10 to 20 cents, and for long-distance calls you need a good supply of 25c pieces. Many large hotels and organisations have free phone numbers, for which you do not need to pay. The code for these is 800. Some hotels also have 'courtesy phones' at airports, which are also free of charge. The STD system is universal but if you do need to contact the operator, dial 0. Instructions on how to use the telephone are clearly printed beside the instrument.

USEFUL WORDS

Although English is spoken throughout the USA, there are some variations in vocabulary which it is essential to know. The following is a brief list of English-American equivalents.

American	English
apartment	flat
balcony	gallery
bathroom/comfort station/rest room	lavatory
check	bill
booth	kiosk
broil	grill
call collect (phone)	reverse charges
candy	sweets
cookies	biscuits
crepes	pancakes
drugstore	chemist
elevator	lift
fabric	material
faucet	tap
flashlight	torch
first floor	ground floor
french fries	chips
gas (gasoline)	petrol
grill	broil
grits (breakfast)	semolina
hashbrowns	fried potatoes
hood (car)	bonnet
jello	jelly
jelly	jam
line	queue
long distance	trunk call
mail	post
mezzanine	dress circle
on the rocks (drinks)	with ice
orchestra	stalls
panty hose	tights
pastrami	peppered beef
pavement	roadway
potato chips	crisps
purse	handbag
sidewalk	pavement
stick shift	gear lever
straight up (drinks)	neat
streetcars	trams
subway	underground
trunk (car)	boot
vest	waistcoat
washcloth	face flannel
wholewheat bread	brown bread
windshield	windscreen

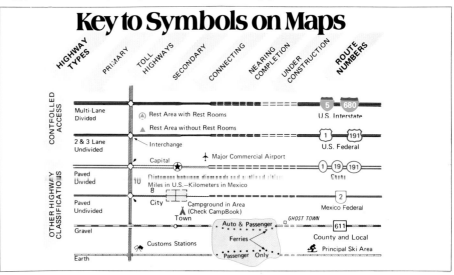

The Bayou State– Louisiana

Colonnaded mansions, quiet bayous, exquisite
flower-garlanded balconies of lacy wrought iron,
jazz, the Mardi Gras festivals, the Mississippi,
voodoo, paddle steamers, magnolia trees and azaleas,
cocktails and Creole cooking – Louisiana is a heady,
romantic mixture of old colonial wealth, tradition,
poverty and innovation born of the French, Spanish
and African cultures which history threw together
beneath a semi-tropical sun.

Although the cotton and sugar-cane plantations
which supported the old landed gentry and throve
on slavery in pre-Civil War days are still an
essential part of Louisiana's economy, it is the huge
oil, gas and sugar refineries along the banks of the
Mississippi and elsewhere which dominate today's
industry. The 20th century, however, struggles hard
to enslave the Louisiana beyond the industrial
centres, and the great river itself cannot shed the
intangible memories of the paddle-steamer days and
the age of Huckleberry Finn.

*The famous steamboats which evolved during the 19th
century to cope with the shallow waters of the
Mississippi were primarily used to transport farmers
and their goods to market. Today, the boats which still
steam up and down 'Ole Man River' are packed with
sightseeing tourists*

ONE INCH— APPROX 90 MILES

Louisiana is an exquisite blend of contrasting cultural influences. French Canadians came here in the middle of the 18th century, when their originally French colony became a British possession. They refused to swear allegiance to the British Crown, and were expelled in 1755. Many went to New England colonies, others back to France, and some took 20 years to find their new homes at the other end of the continent in the French territory of Louisiana. Their descendants, known as Cajuns, retain a culture of their own, and still speak French as their first language.

The Creoles are a people descended from the French-Spanish lineage who formed the elite backbone of the early New Orleans society. Added to these two cultures of European origin are the Africans, whose forebears were the slaves who worked the sugar and cotton plantations of colonial Louisiana. They brought the blues, jazz and voodoo to Louisiana. The American Indian, who was always here, and the Americans, who only arrived on the scene some 180 years ago, complete the pot-pourri of nationalities which, in Louisiana, live together, share their cultures, foods and customs, and above all, seem determined to celebrate life.

It was the Spanish, however, who first set foot on this part of the American continent. In the 16th century, members of Hernando De Soto's expedition discovered the Mis-

sissippi in 1541, while exploring the Arkansas River. A century later, the French became the first serious contenders for supremacy of the region. Travelling in canoes, Robert Cavelier, Sieur de la Salle, and his party, penetrated the heart of the southern states after making their way down the Mississippi from the Great Lakes, via the Illinois River, in 1682. All the land on each side of the Mississippi was claimed in the name of France's King Louis XIV, from whom the state takes its name. It was another 17 years, however, before the first settlement was established 40 miles inland by Pierre le Moyne, Sieur d'Iberville, and the first permanent trading post was established in Natchitoches in 1714. Standing on the Red River, an ideal waterway which feeds both the Mississippi and the Atchafalaya before emptying into the Gulf, Natchitoches remained a prosperous trading centre for 100 years.

Meanwhile, the British having already more than 200 settlers in their colonies on the Eastern seaboard, were taking an increasing interest in the potential of the Gulf region. Though the American War of Independence was still 50 years away, the first of several charismatic characters emerged from the social, political and military scene in Louisiana. Louis Juchereau de St Denis was army commander of Natchitoches, but soon after establishing his fort he faced fierce opposition from the Natchez

The Acadian Village and Tropical Gardens near Lafayette is a restored bayou town which recaptures the lifestyle of the French Acadians during the 1800s

Indians, who wanted revenge for the atrocities the French had perpetrated against their tribe. The decisive battle was at a lake 24 miles south of the town in 1729. The action ended with the Indian tribe being completely annihilated. The carnage earned the lake the name of Sang pour Sang (blood for blood). St Denis, or the Louisiana Cavalier, as he became known, is remembered in an outdoor historical drama presentation performed on a site five miles east of the town on State Route 6.

Two years before St Denis died in 1744, a slave was born into his household who was to become the founder of a family of great wealth and enormous influence. The Melrose plantation, one of scores of magnificent houses still maintained for public view, is the tangible remains of her extraordinary life – extraordinary because it was unheard of at the time that a slave should have the privileges she ultimately enjoyed. The mother of a family of 14, four black, and ten of Franco-African blood, she and her family were sold to a Frenchman. But in 1780, she persuaded him to free her and give her a patch of land. Immediately, she set to work to create what was to become an enormous plantation of tobacco, corn and livestock.

She became so rich that she was able to buy freedom for two of her black children and for one of her grandchildren before she died in 1815. This, and other plantations along the Cane River south of Natchitoches, are open to the public, though access to some is restricted to certain times of the year.

In about 1825, a dramatic and totally unexpected change in the course of the Red River ruined Natchitoches's commercial future. Retreating five miles east, the river left the city high and dry. Fortunately, though the wharves have disappeared, most of the buildings erected in the boom have been preserved. Since then it has earned its keep as a farming centre.

In the latter half of the 18th century, Spain and France played a game of 'pass the parcel' with Louisiana. D'Iberville had recruited his brother, Jean Baptiste le Moyne, Sieur de Bienville, to supervise the Louisiana colony. To Baptiste is given the credit of founding New Orleans in 1718. Then in 1762 France signed the Treaty of Fontainebleau, handing Louisiana to Spain. When Spain took formal possession in 1766 the French and Spanish colonists began to integrate, creating a social and cultural combination whose people became known as the Creoles. They developed a style of living all their own and today their legacy is in the food, the architecture and the proud dignity which generation after generation have sustained.

Meanwhile, the fate of Louisiana was still in the hands of European colonial powers. In 1763, after its defeat in the Seven years War (known in the US as the French and Indian War) France was compelled to relinquish all the provinces of Louisiana east of the Mississippi (except for New Orleans) to the British. In 1783, after the War of Independence, the lands east of the river became American, but the west belonged to Spain as also did Florida. A Spanish treaty, signed on 1st October 1800, handed Louisiana back to France, but it was not to be a happy acquisition for Napoleon. Within three years, in what is known as the Louisi-

ana Purchase, he sold it – this time to the US – for 15 million dollars. Mexico had declared itself independent of Spain, but the boundaries between Mexico and the United States across 2,000 miles of desert remained uncertain.

The influence of the Americans was considered an intrusion by the refined sections of the Creole community, many of whom had demonstrated during the Spanish rule a superior taste in architecture, art and food which even the French, in their turn, respected and did not attempt to change. The impact of the American influx, therefore, was all the more shattering. Louisiana, which reluctantly entered the Union as the 18th state in 1812, just as another war against the British broke out on the American continent, traditionally had little in common with the aspirations of the North. It had even less sympathy for the colonial ambitions of the British; Henry Longfellow poignantly set his epic poem, *Evangeline*, against this background. The poem is said to tell the tragic true love story of a couple who were victims of the colonial conflicts.

Separated by the British in 1755, Emmeline Labiche and Louis Arceneaux, (these are their real names) fled south from Nova Scotia and after many years and numerous harrowing experiences were reunited beneath the Evangeline Oak in St Martinville, a few miles south-west of Lafayette. Unfortunately, as happens in so many genuine love stories, it was not to be a happy ending; on the journey from Acadia, Louis lost his heart to someone else, and when he broke the bad news to Emmeline the shock unhinged her mind, and she died shortly afterwards, hopelessly insane. The tragedy affected the village of St Martinville where many Acadians – refugees from French speaking Canada – had settled. The body of Emmeline Labiche is buried in the

150-year-old St Martin de Tours Catholic Church, one of the oldest churches in the state. A statue to her stands in the churchyard. St Martin's is the second building on the site (the first was put up in 1765) and the French influence is evident in the fascinating replica of the Grotto of Lourdes, copied from a postcard sketch in 1883, and a baptismal font given by Louis XVI. The Acadian House, where Gabriel is said to have lived, has also been preserved. It is now part of a museum which depicts Acadian life in the 18th century, and has

A typical old Cajun home near the Acadian village of St Martinville, on the Bayou Teche

among the exhibits a fully equipped outdoor kitchen and a storehouse of the period. The Evangeline Oak in Port Street, where Evangeline was said to have met with her lover, is claimed to be the most photographed tree in America.

Another town, established by French Acadians and enjoying the legacy of their culture, is Lafayette (see page 20), a few miles north-west of St Martinville. More than 160 years have passed since their forebears emigrated from Nova Scotia, but many of its 78,000 people still speak fluent French. Three miles out of town, the Acadian Village and Tropical Gardens preserve the atmosphere of a bayou town in the late 17th and early 18th centuries. From Lafayette is administered the preservation of one of America's best loved species of trees, the magnificent live oak. Such is their affection for the tree, that the preservation society limits membership to trees at least 100 years old. Membership fees are paid in acorns – 25 acorns admit one tree.

Probably the oldest feature in the whole of Louisiana stands in New Iberia (see page 21), at the corner of Weeks and St Peter Street – a statue of the Roman Emperor Hadrian, sculpted in Rome in about AD 130. The Bayou Teche (the Indian word *teche* means snake) flows by the town, along whose banks the first Acadians from Nova Scotia settled.

Alexandria is a city of 50,000 people, which, with its sister city of Pineville is considered the commercial, educational and military centre of mid-Louisiana. The French and Spanish colonial period is much in evidence at the Kent House State Commemorative Area on Bayou Rapids Road, which contains exquisite examples of Creole cabinet making.

The magnificent and luxurious mansions which, restored and refurbished, hide in vast estates that once were great plantations, are the monuments of an opulent era which came to an end with the Civil War in the last half of the 19th century. One of the most breathtaking examples of a pre-Civil War house (better known as antebellum homes) is at St Francisville, a village about 30 miles north-west of Baton Rouge.

Rosedown Plantation, which has been open to the public since 1964, was one of more than 60 homes built out of gigantic fortunes made from the cotton, sugar-cane and tobacco plantations flourishing in the fertile lower regions of the Mississippi River. More than half of America's millionaires of the mid-1800s founded their wealth on this soil. Rosedown became the home of Daniel and Martha Turnbull, who filled it with treasures from all over the

---

NEW IBERIA

Hotels

BEAU SEJOUR MOTEL: Hwy 182 W, tel 364 4501. 84 rooms. Inexpensive-moderate.

RAMADA INN OF NEW IBERIA: 924 E Admiral Doyle Dr, tel 367 3211. 136 rooms. Expensive.

Places of Interest

SHADOWS-ON-THE-TECHE: 117 E Main St. Restored 1830s mansion originally owned by a wealthy planter. The house and its décor reflect the life-style of a prosperous Louisiana family.

Oakley Plantation House, near St Francisville, where naturalist and painter John James Audubon spent some time as a tutor while working on the unsurpassed Birds of America

ALEXANDRIA

Hotels

HOWARD JOHNSON'S MOTOR LODGE: 700 MacArthur Dr, tel 445 6541. 78 rooms. Expensive.

PLANTATION MOTOR INN: 1919 MacArthur Dr, tel 448 3401. 86 rooms. Moderate-expensive.

SHERATON MOTOR INN ALEXANDRIA: 2716 W MacArthur Dr, tel 487 4261. 127 rooms. Expensive.

Restaurants

PICCADILLY CAFETERIA: 1400 MacArthur Dr, tel 445 0209.

PLANTATION MANOR RESTAURANT: 1919 MacArthur Dr, tel 455 7101. Southern atmosphere and a wide variety of foods. Moderate-expensive.

Places of Interest

ALEXANDRIA ART MUSEUM: 933 Main St. 20th-century arts and crafts.

BRINGHURST PARK: variety of sports facilities and a zoo.

KISATCHIE NATIONAL FOREST: 595,000 acres of Louisiana's only national forest, covering hardwood and cypress swamps with trees festooned in Spanish moss, and sandstone hills clothed in pine woods.

ST FRANCISVILLE

Hotel

HOLIDAY INN: 2 miles N on US 61, tel 635 3821. 100 rooms. Expensive.

Place of Interest

AUDUBON STATE COMMEMORATIVE AREA: 3 miles E off US 61. A 100-acre site containing the Oakley Plantation House. Formerly the home of the naturalist and painter John James Audubon, it is now a museum. Also within the grounds are picnic sites, hiking trails and a visitor centre.

world. Even the gardens, planted with the traditional giant live oaks, were modelled on the great gardens of Paris and Versailles. Martha Turnbull imported camellias, which grow in rich profusion in Louisiana nowadays, and later she brought in azaleas (in Lafayette, a 21-mile azalea trail becomes a stunning path of colour between late February and March every year) and also introduced alternative ideas and plants from Japan.

The largest plantation home in Louisiana, when completed in 1859, was Nottoway, at White Castle, about 18 miles south of Baton Rouge, and a 45-minute drive from New Orleans. The 64-room castle, extending over 53,000 square feet, was built in 1859 in a blend of Greek Revival and Italian styles. It was nearly destroyed in the Civil War, but was saved by a former guest of the mansion who happened to be the gunboat officer in charge of a detachment of Union forces sent to blow the place up.

Oak Alley, which takes its name from an avenue of oaks a quarter of a mile long, was a French sugar planter's wedding present for his new bride. Like Nottoway, it was spared the ravages of the Civil War and survives as a fine example of 18th-century architecture, thanks to Andrew and Josephine Stewart, who had it restored in 1925, lived in it and turned the place into a non-profit making foundation. Now visitors flock to it, joining conducted tours of the house led by the Stewart family's old retainers – some have been in their service for more than 25 years. Oak Alley is at Vacherie, about 30 miles south-east of Baton Rouge along State Route 18, the Great River Road, along which several other famous houses are situated beside the Mississippi.

BATON ROUGE

Hotels

ALAMO PLAZA HOTEL COURTS: 4243 Florida Blvd, tel 924 7231. 97 rooms. Inexpensive-moderate.

BATON ROUGE HILTON: Corporate Sq, tel 924 5000. 305 rooms. Expensive.

BEST WESTERN CAPITOL HOUSE: Convention St, tel 383 7721. 300 rooms. Expensive.

Restaurants

JACK SABIN'S RESTAURANT: 9716 Airline Hwy, tel 926 0565. Well-prepared food with plenty of variety. Cocktail lounge. Moderate.

THE VILLAGE RESTAURANT: 8464 Airline Hwy, tel 925 2081. Attractive dining-rooms serving excellent Italian and American food. Strict dress code. Moderate.

Places of Interest – See tour page 19

Oak Alley Plantation, outside Vacherie, is named after this magnificent avenue of live oaks.

Captain H M Shreve's snagboat 'Aid', with which he cleared the Great Raft, a 160-mile log jam on the Red River near Shreveport

SHREVEPORT

Hotels

DAYS INN-BOSSIER CITY: 200 John Wesley Blvd, tel 742 9200. 178 rooms. Inexpensive.

REGENCY MOTOR HOTEL: 102 Lake St, tel 222 7717. 148 rooms. Expensive.

SHERATON BOSSIER INN: 2015 Old Minden Rd, tel 742 9700. 219 rooms. Moderate.

Restaurants

BROCATO'S RESTAURANT: 189 E Kings Hwy, tel 865 2352. Excellent steaks, seafood and Italian specialities. Cocktails. Children's menu. Moderate.

SANSONE'S RESTAURANT: 701 E Kings Hwy, tel 865 5146. Good variety of steak dishes, plus Italian cooking and seafood. Children's menu. Entertainment. Moderate.

Places of Interest

BARNWELL MEMORIAL GARDEN AND ART CENTER: 501 River Pkwy, tel 226 6495. Shreveport's delightful botanical gardens.

CROSS LAKE: Source of the city's water supply. A local beauty spot, especially in March when the red-bud trees are in bloom. Boating and fishing available.

R W NORTON ART GALLERY: 4700 block, Creswell Av. Houses examples of both European and American painting and sculpture.

STATE EXHIBIT MUSEUM: 3015 Greenwood Rd. The building specialises in murals and displays depicting Louisiana industry, natural resources and agricultural life. An art gallery shows the work of local painters.

his own design, he moved a 160-mile jam of driftwood from the Red River which had prevented traffic from breaking through into the north-west reaches of the river. The free movement of ships which followed certainly changed the economic outlook of the state. On many of the waterfront stretches, the warehouses have been restored to their Victorian splendour. During the Civil War Shreveport briefly became the capital of Louisiana, and though it could justifiably claim to have crushed the Union advance in the last Confederate victory of the war at nearby Mansfield, it was also the place where the last Confederate Army surrendered. A more recent Louisiana hero is also Baton Rouge's most revered local figure. Though he was born at Winnfield several hundred miles north-west of the city, Huey P Long belonged to the capital, and was Louisiana's most unorthodox states-

Baton Rouge (see page 19) has been the state capital since the end of the Civil War, and is the nation's seventh largest port. The city, characterised by magnolias and calm lakes, encapsulates Louisiana's cosmopolitan character. It is said that ten flags have flown over Baton Rouge, including the Union Jack, the Tricolour of France, the Stars and Stripes, an early flag of the United States, the Spanish flag and the flag of the Confederate states, Independent Louisiana, and the West Florida Lone Star.

During the Civil War Louisiana showed where her allegiance properly belonged. The glorious era of good living and style, threatened by the conflict between the states, encouraged Louisiana to leave the Union in 1861, and join the Confederacy two months later. It was not to be re-admitted to the Union until 1868. The war, however, destroyed much of the fabric of Louisiana's life. Baton Rouge escaped most of the fighting, although there is a monument to a two-hour battle fought within the city limits on the 5 August 1862.

Some of the most decisive Civil War battles were at Shreveport, on the western side of the state. Now the third largest city in Louisiana, Shreveport, situated on the Red River, is named after Captain Henry Miller Shreve, Louisiana's greatest folk hero. For it was this veteran of the 19th-century steam boats – he was a master navigator on the Mississippi – who in 1833 did the impossible. Using a 'snagboat' of

man. One of his greatest achievements was, by sheer force of personality and determination, to have the Louisiana State Capitol built. Completed in March 1932 on a 20-acre site, the 34-storey-high marble edifice was the culmination of five years of controversy during which time he set out to change the established order, and to improve the condition of ordinary people. A spell-binding orator and debater, he became governor of the state and a United States Senator. During his terms of public office, he is credited with introducing paved roads and free school books to the state. Quick-witted and extremely confident of his abilities, he started out to become a lawyer and took a law degree in eight months! Ironically, it was at the State Capitol – the fulfilment of his life's ambition – that he met his death. Visiting the place he so loved, on Sunday, 8 September

1935, he was shot on the first floor by an assassin. He died two days later. A bronze statue which stands at the head of his grave facing the capitol is lit by spotlight at night. Another memorial is at his birthplace at Winnfield, a salt-mining, limestone quarrying and lumbering centre. He also has two famous bridges named after him – one at Baton Rouge and the other in New Orleans.

Certainly, Long helped to push Louisiana into the 20th century. The state now has a population of nearly 4 million and a territory covering nearly 51,000 square miles of which over 3,000 are under water. In fact, Louisiana is so full of bayous (creeks),

The bayous of Louisiana, rich in plant and animal life, are stretches of water which have wandered away from, or have been left behind by a slow-flowing main river

many of them bearing French or Indian names, that there are some 7,000 miles of navigable waterways in the state. The hundreds of square miles of marshes are also a haven for wildlife.

Fishing is a popular sport in the Toledo Bend Reservoir through which the Louisiana and Texas boundary runs, and in the Atchafalaya Swamp near the mouth of the river. This is the second largest swamp wilderness in the United States (first is the Everglades in Florida) and is still the last undrained river basin swamp in the Mississippi Valley. Major saltwater game fish are tarpon, mackerel, red snapper and pompano. While the coastal marshlands produce speckled trout and red fish among other species, freshwater fish include white perch – locally known as crappie – bass, bream and catfish. Louisiana, in all its variety, is unlikely to disappoint.

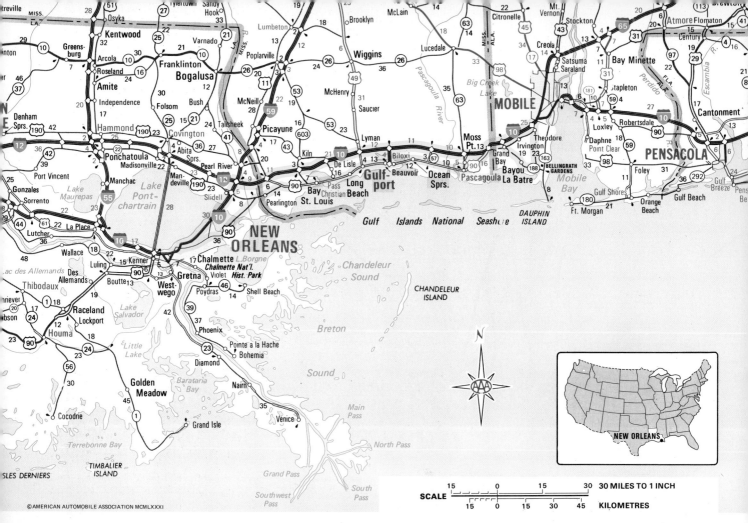

SCALE

15   0   15   30   **30 MILES TO 1 INCH**

15   0   15   30   45   **KILOMETRES**

The Mississippi Coast

2 days – around 300 miles

New Orleans – Bellingrath Gardens – Mobile – Pascagoula – Ocean Springs – Biloxi – Beauvoir – Gulfport – New Orleans.

Leave New Orleans on Interstate 10 and after about 110 miles connect with State Route 188 at Grand Bay. Continue east for 15 miles on State Route 188, then north on County Route 59 to Bellingrath Gardens.

Bellingrath Gardens

Azaleas flower from February to April, followed by dogwood, spirea and mountain laurel. Hydrangeas and gardenias steal the scene in May while countless annuals bloom throughout the summer. Camellias take over from September through to April, with chrysanthemums as strong competition until December. All year round the gardens are ablaze with colour, where once untamed tropical jungle grew. The landscaped acres still retain the primitive jungle air, though paths and bridges enable visitors to explore even the remotest corners of the gardens, which were created with the assistance of English, French and American landscape architects.

The brick and wrought-iron mansion displays the Bessie Morse Bellingrath collection of antique furniture, precious china, crystal, silver and oriental rugs.

Drive north on County Route 59 to US 90 and Interstate 10 for the 20 miles to Mobile.

Mobile

This is Alabama's only seaport, an internationally important and almost landlocked harbour lying on the west side of the sheltered 27-mile-long Mobile Bay. Although eight miles across, the entrance to the bay is protected by Dauphin Island and the Gulf Shores peninsula. One of the largest dry docks and shipbuilding centres along the Gulf, this is where many of America's ships were constructed, converted or repaired during World War II. Today the vast natural harbour and the extensive docks attract the major industries of oil refining, chemicals, paper-making and food processing.

Mobile was originally settled by the Mobila Indians from whom it gained its name. In 1702 Sieur de Bienville founded the city for the French, and as the first permanent white settlement in Alabama, it served as the capital of the French colonial empire until 1719. The English took over in 1763, followed by the Spanish in 1780. Finally the United States took possession in 1813, though peace was still hard to come by, for Mobile again became a battlefield in the Civil War when Confederate and Federal troops fought for possession during the 1860s. The Federal forces were eventually victorious in 1864, besieging the surrounding forts and forcing the Confederates to surrender.

Much of the atmosphere of the Old South still persists in Mobile, but the stamp of the early French settlers is seen in the colourful Mardi Gras Festival which begins here in late November and reaches its climax during the two weeks before Ash Wednesday.

Three of the forts steeped in the history of the early struggles for Mobile are open to the public. In the city itself, occupying Royal and Church streets, is Fort Condé, which was used successively by French, Spanish, English and American troops. It has been restored to appear as it did during the occupation by the French in 1735. The museum it houses traces the fort's history. Fort Gaines, one of the fortifications guarding Mobile Bay during the Civil War, is on Dauphin Island, where the French settled before moving to the mainland. The island, now a boating and fishing haven with splendid beaches is reached by ferry, a temporary arrangement set up since 1979, when Hurricane Frederick destroyed the bridge which linked the island to the mainland. Mobile Point, at the tip of the Gulf Shores peninsular is the site of Fort Morgan. This fort shared strategic importance with Fort Gaines during the Civil War. A Confederate stronghold, it surrendered in 1864 after an 18-day siege following the Battle of Mobile Bay. The fort museum gives the full history.

A star attraction, just over 2 miles east of the city, and reached through the Bankhead tunnel, is the USS *Alabama* Battleship Memorial, dedicated to the veterans of Alabama. Visitors may tour the decks, turrets, berthing and messing compartments, captain's cabin, bridge and wardroom. You can also visit the torpedo room and crews' quarters on the USS *Drum*, a submarine docked alongside.

Museums abound in Mobile, all of them free. On Government Street, in a restored 1872 townhouse, is the Museum of the City of Mobile, which contains exhibits portraying the history of the seaport, and also preserves a unique collection of horse-drawn vehicles. The firefighting history of the city is featured at the Phoenix Fire Museum on Claiborne Street. A collection of American and African art and a contemporary crafts display are on view at the Fine Arts Museum of the South in Langan Park on Museum Drive.

Impressive 19th-century houses are a characteristic of Mobile. Good examples are the Richards D A R House in De Tonti Square and the splendid Oakleigh Museum at Oakleigh Place, which was built by slaves in 1833. Both houses contain authentic period furnishings and Civil War relics.

The most spectacular church in the city is the Catholic Cathedral of the Immaculate Conception, on Claiborne Street, but this is eclipsed by the amazing Greek Orthodox Malbis Memorial Church about 12 miles east of the city off US 90, at Malbis. This faithful copy of a Byzantine church

in Athens contains exquisite mosaics and murals.

Bienville Square in the business area, is one of many beautiful parks renowned for its bush azaleas and live oaks. In opposite corners of the square are, significantly, a French cannon from Fort Condé and an English cannon from Fort Charlotte. Many of the city's other floral attractions are linked together by the 35-mile flower-lined Azalea Trail, which winds through the city's residential areas. The trail is indicated by pink lines and signs.

The Bellingrath Gardens cover 800 acres of beautifully landscaped grounds

Hotels

BEST WESTERN ADMIRAL SEMMES MOTOR HOTEL: 250 Government St, tel 432 4441. 106 rooms. Expensive.

HOWARD JOHNSON'S MOTOR LODGE: 3132 Government Blvd, tel 471 2402. 160 rooms. Expensive.

TAYLOR MOTEL: 2598 Government Blvd, tel 479 5481. 47 rooms. Moderate.

Restaurants

BERNARD'S: 407 Conti St, tel 432 5176. Dine in style in a historic mansion of the Old South. Moderate-expensive.

WINTZELL'S OYSTER HOUSE: 605 Dauphin St, tel 433 1004. Colourful, casual atmosphere. Oysters and local seafood the speciality. Inexpensive-moderate.

Drive west on Interstate 10 for 30 miles and join US 90 for 12 miles to Pascagoula.

Pascagoula

Tourism, fishing and industry have replaced lumber as the chief money spinners in this old town on the Pascagoula River. The Indian tribe, from whom the town and river take their name, committed mass suicide in the river, by walking hand in hand into its waters. They drowned themselves rather than accept certain and ignoble defeat at the hands of the warlike Biloxi Indians. The Pascagoula River is

called the 'singing river', because it is said that on quiet summer evenings the death chant of the Pascagoulas can still be heard.

Old Spanish Fort on Krebs Lake, just off US 90, was in fact built by the French in 1718, but was later captured by the Spanish. It is one of the oldest structures still standing in the Mississippi Valley. A museum with interesting relics is open daily in the fort.

Continue west for 19 miles on US 90, the Old Spanish Trail, for Ocean Springs.

Shrimp boats docked in the harbour at Pascagoula. The Gulf coast is one of the richest shrimping grounds in the USA

As a mark of respect, the citizens of Biloxi painted this lighthouse black when President Abraham Lincoln was assassinated in 1865

captured the settlement in 1719 and moved its location. It became capital of the French territory of Louisiana until 1723 when New Orleans took over the role. Since then several European kings have laid claim to the city, leaving a legacy of fascinating cultures and customs.

Shrimp and oyster-fishing provide an important income for the locals here, and every June the shrimp fleet is blessed during a colourful ceremony. You can discover more by taking the hour-long Shrimp Tour Train which leaves Biloxi Lighthouse on US 90. A tape recording outlines the history and events which have shaped the city. Alternatively, a Harbour Tour leaves the small craft harbour at the foot of Main Street. This hour-and-a-half spectacular sightseeing and trawling expedition aboard the *Sailfish* includes on-the-spot identification of the catch by experts. Boat trips are also available from this harbour to Ship Island aboard the *Pan American Clipper*.

Near the end of Benashi Avenue off West Beach Boulevard is Old Lighthouse, built in 1848. The lens of the lighthouse was removed and buried during the Civil War so that the light could not guide the Union forces to the city. A mother and daughter operated the light unaided for 62 years following the Civil War.

Continue west for over 5 miles along US 90 to Beauvoir.

elegant house dating from 1853 and a quaint cottage, where Davis wrote the *Rise and Fall of the Confederate Government*. Many of his books are still in the cottage which served him as a study and a library. The old Confederate soldiers' Hospital now houses the Old South Museum which displays a wealth of Civil War relics.

Drive west along the Old Spanish Trail for 17 miles to Gulfport.

Gulfport
The Gulfport of miles of sparkling beaches and pleasant boulevards, set in a beautiful countryside easily toured by car, and the Gulfport of the busy seaport concerned solely with the shipping of timber, fish and cotton are world's apart, yet both fascinating to visit. Fishing can be both business and pleasure, and the annual Mississippi Deep Sea Fishing Rodeo, held here for three days in early July, is a magnet for competitors from all over the USA.

The *Pan American Clipper* also operates a service from Gulfport to Ship Island. Twelve miles south of the town, the island guards the entrance to Biloxi Bay. Ruined Fort Massachusetts was the centre of Civil War struggles and has a stormy history of capture and recapture. To the Union it was an important link in the naval blockade of the south, and many Confederates were flung into its dungeons.

Return to New Orleans by following the Old Spanish Trail westwards along 11 miles of dazzling white beaches to Pass Christian. Here cross a scenic causeway and drive for 25 miles to Pearlington. Cross the Pearl River, then continue west across the mouth of Lake Pontchartrain to New Orleans.

Ocean Springs
Artists and craftsmen have adopted this attractive Gulf resort in recent years, and have given it the casual and unhurried air of an artists' colony. Established by d'Iberville in 1699, who built Fort Maurepas on this site, Ocean Springs was the first permanent European settlement in the Mississippi Valley. You can enjoy good cuisine here at Trilby's, where seafood and Creole fare are specialities.

Drive west for about 3 miles along US 90 and cross Back Bay to Biloxi.

Biloxi
One of the most delightful cities and one of the oldest settlements in the Gulf, Biloxi is built on a narrow peninsula bordered by the Gulf of Mexico, Biloxi Bay and Back Bay. Old stucco cottages and vast moss-laden oaks lend a sense of timelessness to the city's streets, perfumed by the magnolia and camellia blossoms which thrive in the mild and pleasant climate. A drive along Beach Boulevard gives

an unforgettable view of the beautiful coast.

The original site of Biloxi (the name means 'first people') was across the bay, settled by Biloxi Indians in 1699. The French

Beauvoir
The last home of Jefferson Davis, President of the Confederacy, is the main attraction here. The grounds are maintained as a Confederate shrine and include an

Gulfport, a major port on the Gulf coast, has become a popular centre for boat-owners and yachtsmen

A Taste of the Old South

2 days – 335 miles

New Orleans – Plaquemine – Baton Rouge – Lafayette – St Martinville – Avery Island – New Iberia – Thibodaux – Houma – Chalmette National Historical Park – New Orleans

Leave New Orleans on Interstate 10 driving for 40 miles to State Route 70 crossing the Mississippi River to State Route 1. Continue north on State Route 1 for about 20 miles to Plaquemine.

Plaquemine
The most fascinating feature of this small town is the Chapel of the Madonna between Point Pleasant and Bayou Goula on State Route 168. Only six feet by eight feet, it contains an altar and five chairs, with just enough room to accommodate a priest and an acolyte during mass. An Italian immigrant built the chapel single-handed in the hope that the Virgin Mary would cure his desperately ill child.

Bayou Goula is a typical sleepy blue 'bayou' – a stretch of water which has been left behind by the slow-flowing Mississippi. Filled with swamp grass and inhabited by alligators, the bayous of Acadiana meander from Lafayette down to the Gulf coast forcing highways to take a sinuous path.

The Carriage Museum on Martin Street is packed with exhibits of local interest. Also worth a visit is the City Hall, built in 1849, which was originally the parish courthouse.

Drive north for about 10 miles on State Route 1 to Baton Rouge

Baton Rouge
Winding drives, magnolias, splendid 19th-century homes and peaceful bayous are the essential ingredients of this most elegant of cities, the capital of Louisiana. Although overshadowed by world-famous New Orleans, it is a thriving commercial centre and a bustling seaport, where the largest ocean-going vessels can be accommodated in its docks, and locally grown sugar-cane is the

Formal gardens in Baton Rouge seen from the top of the State Capitol

principal export. English, French and Spanish influences linger from the city's chequered past, creating a cosmopolitan town typical of colourful Louisiana.

Thirty-four storeys above pleasant, formal gardens, is the observation tower of America's tallest State Capitol. The dramatic view from the top, of Baton Rouge hugging the banks of the lazy Mississippi, serves as an excellent introduction to the city. You can also see the spot on the first floor where Huey P Long, Governor of Louisiana when the capitol was built, was assassinated. Other attractions include the splendid Marble Hall, murals, statuary and bas-relief on huge brass doors. Huey Long's grave lies in the grounds and has a statue of him beside it.

The Gothic-style Old State Capitol is on Lafayette Street and North Boulevard. Built in 1847, it was burned by the Union Army, but was later repaired and used until 1932. It resembles a Norman Castle and contains a vast spiral staircase which winds up to an unusual stained-glass dome. At the base of the staircase is the Baton Rouge Tourist Information Centre. The old Senate and House chambers display excellent exhibits of contemporary art.

Across the lake from the capitol is the Governor's Mansion, built in 1963 as a replica of an opulent plantation mansion. Tours around the house can be arranged by appointment and are free of charge.

In 1930 the ill-fated Huey Long built the Old Governor's Mansion Museum, now the Louisiana Arts and Science Center. Each room is

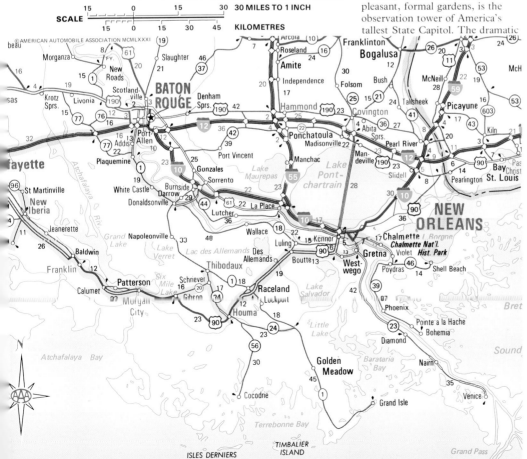

dedicated to one particular governor of Louisiana. Adjacent to the museum on North Boulevard is a planetarium. Also a part of the Center is the Riverside Museum, housed in a fine old railway station by the river. A model on display illustrates the channel changes which have occurred in the Mississippi. An excellent restaurant here specialises in Creole cuisine. Vintage railway relics, including a 1918 steam engine, are on display next to the museum.

The nation's largest predominantly Black university, Southern University, is perched high above the Mississippi. Three miles south of the city is the Louisiana State University Campus at Nicholson Avenue. An information centre is at the base of Memorial Tower at the centre of the campus. There are a number of free museums here which include the Anglo-American Art Museum in Memorial Tower; a Museum of Science in Foster Hall, which highlights the natural history of Louisiana; and the Geoscience Museum, which occupies four floors and exhibits Indian folklore relics and archaeological finds from the historic Bayou Jasmin site.

From the wealth of lavish, colonnaded southern plantation homes in the area, it is difficult to select one for special mention. Only 5 minutes from the city on Highland Road is Mount Hope Plantation, considered to be one of Louisiana's best restorations. Built in 1817, it is beautifully furnished in the Federal Sheraton and Empire periods. Accommodation is offered here. What better way to end a packed day of sightseeing in this fascinating southern city?

Continue west on Interstate 10 for 53 miles to Lafayette.

Lafayette
The undisputed heart of Acadiana, this city is full of mementoes to the first wave of French exiles who arrived here from Acadia in Nova Scotia in 1755.

The life of these early exiles is reflected at the Acadian Village and Tropical Gardens 3 miles south of Interstate 10, following signs to Scott. This is a bayou town which has been relocated and restored. You can stroll through the town and see the general store, a blacksmith's shop, a trading post and a number of houses which are open to view. The chapel at New Hope in the centre is a fund-raising focus for the Alleman Center for Louisiana's handicapped citizens. The tropical gardens are also a part of the Alleman Center and display plants from all the hot areas of the world.

Back in the city, Lafayette Museum on Lafayette Street contains period furnishings, heirlooms and Mardi Gras costumes. In March and April Lafayette is the scene of the Azalea Trail festivities, when plantation homes throughout the region are open to the public.

For recommended hotels see page 11

Leave Lafayette south on US 90 for 11 miles then take State Route 96 for about 4 miles to St Martinville.

St Martinville
St Martinville was settled in the 18th century by Acadians and French refugees, and is today one of the oldest and most charming of the small towns in Louisiana. Many aristocratic French settlers fashioned St Martinville into a centre of elegant living and culture. Balls and operas were attended by impeccably dressed notables and the town earned the name 'La petit Paris'. It is steeped in tributes to Longfellow's fictitious Acadian princess, Evangeline.

Evangeline Oak close to the bayou at the end of Port Street has probably been photographed more than any other tree in the world. The ill-fated princess (see page 11) is reputed to have docked her boat here when she arrived at the end of her journey from Nova Scotia.

The Longfellow-Evangeline State Commemorative Area is on State Route 31, bordered by the Bayou Teche. Displays of Acadian life and coats and arms of the French aristocracy are on view in the Acadian House Museum said to have been occupied by Louis Arceneaux, the 'Gabriel' of Longfellow's poem *Evangeline*. The Cajun Cabin is a novel gift shop and there are picknicking areas, camping facilities, a restaurant and a swimming pool in the grounds.

Drive south on State Route 31 7 miles to State Route 329 in New Iberia; then continue for 7 miles south on the same route, over a toll bridge to Avery Island.

Avery Island
The oldest rock salt mine in the Western Hemisphere is to be found on this island which is underlaid by a salt dome. In parts the salt lies within 12 feet of the surface. The island is also the home of Tabasco sauce, created by Edward Avery McIlhenny, who used the fiery local peppers in his secret recipe. His descendants now run the old factory, and though free guided tours are available, the recipe still remains a secret.

The Jungle Gardens and Bird Sanctuary off State Route 329 are

The Riverside Museum, Baton Rouge, at the old Illinois Central station. Exhibits are wide-ranging, and include this steam locomotive

sadly not open to the public, is the supremely beautiful plantation mansion Rienzi, dating from 1796.

Drive south-west on State Route 24 for about 12 miles to Houma.

Houma

Shrimps and oysters taken from the Gulf waters are the mainstay of this town on the Intracoastal Canal. Local seafood-packing plants are on view to the public during mornings from May to July and you can tour the US Sugar Cane Experimental Station on weekdays if you make an appointment.

Drive east for about 62 miles on US 90 to New Orleans and take State Route 46 for about 10 miles south-east to Chalmette National Historical Park.

Chalmette National Historical Park

Chalmette battlefield marks the site of the last bitter struggle between American and British forces which took place on 8th January 1815. Westward expansion of the United States followed and General Andrew Jackson became a national hero and ultimately president. British casualties numbered nearly 2,000. The visitors' centre at Beauregard Plantation House supplies information on the strategies of the famous battle, including an audiovisual programme. A battlefield tour includes Chalmette National Cemetery.

Retrace your path along State Route 46 and follow signs for downtown New Orleans.

The colonnaded façade of Shadows-on-the-Teche, a mansion in New Iberia

Chalmette National Historical Park – a battlefield and Beauregard House

a legacy of the famous Edward Avery McIlhenny. Here 300 acres of beautifully landscaped grounds display exotic blooms, a Chinese Garden complete with a Buddha nearly 1,000 years old and a bird sanctuary with a famous rookery of egrets. Herons visit the sanctuary in summer and wild fowl shelter here in winter.

Return north on State Route 329 over the toll bridge and follow signs to New Iberia.

New Iberia

Bordering the romantic Bayou Teche, New Iberia experienced a population explosion in the 1830s when the town became the terminus for steamboats travelling up the bayou from New Orleans. Now a very prosperous town, it is the centre of the sugar-cane industry. The present population is descended from the Spanish, French and Acadians who established the town around 1835. Known as the 'Sugar Bowl' of Louisiana, stately old mansions abound in the area, several of

which are owned and maintained by the National Trust for Historical Preservation.

Shadows-on-the-Teche is a marvellous vintage 1830 plantation on Main Street, in the heart of the town. The house furnishings typify the lifestyle of five generations of a wealthy mid 19th-century Louisiana family. An exquisite garden of camellias, orchids and roses is set amidst moss-draped trees, and a smooth lawn sweeps down to the Bayou Teche.

Follow US 90 for 62 miles to the small town of Gibson, then take State Route 20 to Thibodaux 30 miles away. West of Thibodaux is the heart of the Bayou Country where highways are very labyrinthine. You will need a detailed road map.

Thibodaux

The first trading post established between New Orleans and Bayou Teche, this sugar-belt town on Bayou Lafourche was incorporated in 1838.

Visible across the bayou, but

New Orleans

There is no other city quite like New Orleans in all of the USA. It has been dubbed 'The city that care forgot', and in that phrase lies the key to its distinctive character.

Lying on a deep bend of America's largest river, the Mississippi, the city was founded by the French, who sold it to the Spanish (who sold it back again), and was finally bought by the Americans from Napoleon.

Throughout its history, New Orleans has cherished the French Quarter. Here, among the delightful architecture for which the city is renowned, the elegant Creole culture which shaped early New Orleans took root, and has since remained a distinctive force behind its fortunes, developing a particular identity of its own.

From these beginnings stems New Orleans' appeal, its warmth, colour and above all, hospitality. Nothing expresses the elated mood of this city more than the extraordinary festival time culminating in Mardi Gras, and the constant, energetic output of jazz, the music New Orleans created and which expresses the city's flamboyant mood.

▼ *St Louis Cathedral and the statue of Andrew Jackson in New Orleans' Jackson Square*

▶ *The mecca of the jazz enthusiast – Preservation Hall in St Peter Street, where jazz is found in its purest form*

New Orleans seems to bring out the best in its people. Holding festivals, joining parades and throwing parties are a part of the New Orleans' way of life. Certainly, the combination of peoples and cultures the centuries have brought to the city has created a unique style of living and a magical if indefinable atmosphere.

The particular attraction in this city is the French Quarter, or Vieux Carré, which to many *is* New Orleans. To ignore the rest of the city, however, is a mistake, but it is true that the French Quarter packs enough atmosphere, sights and entertainments within the 70 blocks or so it occupies to make further exploration seem irrelevant.

The narrow streets and old buildings, embellished by the ornate filigree patterns of the wrought iron railings and the balconies of exquisite workmanship; the beautiful, flower-garden courtyards sometimes glimpsed behind massive gates or down alleyways, are more reminiscent of a great European city than of an American port. World-famous Bourbon Street is New Orleans's Strip. Although the porn merchants have moved in, they have become part of the city's street culture. The aroma of exotic foods, the clamour of chords on a tinkling piano, the laughter and the bellowing voices of doorway barkers, give Bourbon Street a sense of excitement that makes the pulse race. At night it adopts an almost Victorian naughty nineties air. Nearby Royal Street is a little quieter, for its numerous antique shops, windows ablaze with glittering *objets d'art*, exquisite glassware, furniture and prints, are closed.

Wherever you are in the French Quarter, you are never far from jazz. The lazy beat underpinning a soaring saxophone or trumpet, beckons from doorways and windows. Jazz was born in New Orleans, and is still played here with a freshness and verve unequalled anywhere in the world, often by men who were among the first to play it. Call in at Preservation Hall, in St Peter Street, where an unprepossessing doorway leads to a small room in which the top exponents of jazz gather to play pure, traditional jazz to a generally young, totally mesmerized audience overflowing into the corridor and street. It has been like that for more than 50 years, and although the individuals have changed, the band and the audiences are in essence the same. Or try Al Hirt at his place in Bourbon Street. Like Buddy Bolden, Nick La Rocca, Jelly Roll Morton or – best-known to the modern generation of all – Louis Armstrong, Al Hirt is the doyen of New Orleans in the true tradition of the great jazz men of the past. The pleasures of good eating and drinking are just a step or two away.

You can find a muted corner for drink and conversation next door to a foot-stomping, sawdust-strewn bar, and enjoy the atmosphere in each equally. You can eat ten or more courses at dinner in any one of a dozen famous New Orleans restaurants, or sit at a bar like Felix's in Iberville Street, eating raw oysters with a side order of mustard sauce for next to nothing. Even expensive restaurants are not outrageously so.

To sit with a drink at hand in the courtyard at Brennan's in Royal Street waiting for a candlelit table, with time to look at the splendour of the décor

in ground-floor rooms and on the balconies, is not as extravagant a way to spend an evening as it may seem, nor is the menu comparatively as pricey as many similar establishments in Europe.

Or try Galatoire's, in Bourbon Street, which like Brennan's serves exquisite Creole French cuisine: both are two of America's finest restaurants.

One of the great charms of New Orleans is that such standards of excellence are not only to be found in the tourist areas. Across Canal Street, one of the widest thoroughfares in the States, lies the other half of downtown New Orleans – the Garden District. Here, too, the atmosphere in some of the streets is enhanced by the splendour of the shops and the hotels, restaurants, and houses.

Not as ribald or excessive as some parts of the French Quarter, the Garden District has an air of restrained dignity. The Caribbean Room of the Pontchartrain Hotel (Pontchartrain was the name of Louis XIV's Minister of the Marine) in St Charles Avenue is one of the South's great temples to fine living. The rich, maroon carpets and chandeliers match the atmosphere of discreet elegance. The Creole French cuisine is renowned for its subtle

flavours. But best-known is the Caribbean Room's arch-folly – the Mile High Pecan Pie. It is a concoction of pecan nuts, ice cream, toasted meringue and bitter sweet chocolate sauce. It earned its name because it stands nearly a foot high on a plate. It is also best shared with someone else, for, as the last course of a meal, it usually defeats the most persistent appetite.

The Garden District also has fine antique shops and museums – Magazine Street is a good place to wander and window-shop. The District is mainly the dormitory of some of the well-to-do families whose ancestors helped to build the business section of the city after its purchase by the USA.

The influx of the American community in the 18th-century after the Louisiana Purchase (see page 11), helped New Orleans to exploit the wealth under its feet, and the cluster of skyscrapers and modern glass-faced offices which at first sight seem out of keeping with the character of the city, are the result of their endeavours. The Americans' hard-nosed methods did nothing to endear the newcomers to the Spanish, French and Cajun communities. Already having ruled, abandoned and repossessed the city the

▲ *Royal Street, in the French Quarter, is renowned for its antique shops*

◄ *The bright lights of Bourbon Street*

► *Old and new architecture in New Orleans. The 18th-century spire of St Louis Cathedral is dwarfed by one of the city's modern skyscrapers*

▼ *The steamboat 'Natchez', docked at Toulouse Street Wharf, and the Greater New Orleans Bridge*

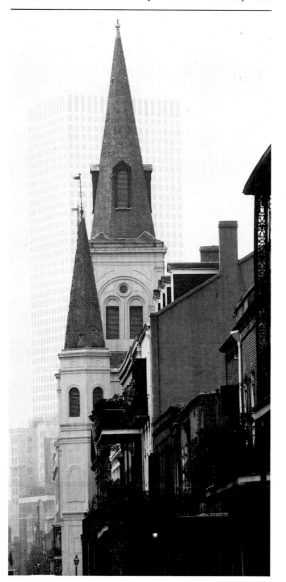

French left an indelible mark on its architecture, food and culture.

The Spanish, too, had made an enduring impression in the centuries of their influence on New Orleans. So when the Americans arrived, all brash and business-like, conflicts quickly arose. Eventually, rather than integrate with the Creoles, the Americans built their own homes on the other side of 'the track', once the Mississippi Canal, and now Canal Street.

The French claim to New Orleans was irrefutable. In the 18th century, 19 years after his brother had established the first settlement in Louisiana for Louis XIV (see page 10), Jean Baptiste Le Moyne, Sieur d'Iberville and Sieur de Bienville, acting for the Regent of France, the Duc d'Orléans, surveyed the swampy banks in the bend of the river and decided it was the place to found New Orleans. A year later, with the help of 80 hardy sailors, the riverbank was drained and the French Quarter began to arise. Soon, the Creoles settled in large numbers, but after two disastrous fires which razed the French Quarter to the ground in 1788 and 1794, the Spanish rebuilt the Quarter. Thus, many of the buildings standing today are not of French design at all, even though the French street names have been retained.

Although no British influence is discernible in New Orleans, it was on the doorstep of the city that the Battle of New Orleans in 1815 finally put paid to British aspirations. Fought at Chalmette, to the east of the city, it was to be the last important land engagement between the United States and Great Britain. A national historic park commemorates the battlefield.

General Andrew Jackson, at the head of 4,000 militia, repelled a British assault on the east bank of the Mississippi River, inflicting some 2,000 casualties for the loss of only seven killed and six wounded. The victory eventually earned Andrew Jackson the presidency of the country. A statue in his honour in Jackson Square in the heart of the French Quarter shows him seated on a prancing horse. The sculptor is believed to have achieved for the first time the difficult task of depicting a horse with two hooves off the ground at the same time. (Andrew Jackson also has a rather fine restaurant named after him in Royal Street in the French Quarter).

Even the pirate, Jean Lafitte, who headed a motley band of Creoles, Negro slaves and Indians into the battle, has been honoured, and Lafitte's Blacksmith Shop in Bourbon Street, which served as a front for his smuggling operations, now houses a tavern.

Jackson Square is well worth visiting for several important landmarks. The Spanish seat of Government was housed at the Cabildo, and the Presbytere is the home of the Louisiana State Musuem. With its triple steeples, St Louis Cathedral is one of the oldest cathedrals still in use in America. The present basilica dates back to 1794. It was dedicated as a Cathedral on Christmas Eve – 16 days after it was nearly destroyed in the second great fire of New Orleans. The first fire completely razed the original church. St Anthony's Garden, behind the church, was at one time a notorious duelling ground.

The Pontalba buildings flanking Jackson Square are claimed to be the first purpose-built apartment houses in America. Erected in 1849, the red-brick buildings, designed in Renaissance-style, became one of the most desirable addresses in town. Part of the Louisiana State Museum is now housed there. The square, once a parade ground for the French and Spanish armies, is a kaleidoscope of colour and movement as crowds converge on it from early morning to late at night. Although tourists are much in evidence, Jackson Square is a place where New Orleans residents also like to go. On any one day, a conjurer, a child dancer, or even a performing dog can make up the impromptu entertainment.

Here one can find evidence of the indefinable quality of New Orleans, described by the Cajun word, *lagniappe* (pronounced lan-y-ap). It expresses an act of goodwill, friendliness, or generosity (a little gift pushed into the wrapping of a purchase at a shop, or an extra oyster or two with an order of a dozen at a bar), and is usually accompanied by a deprecating shrug of the shoulders. It also explains why New Orleans has such a record of bizarre achievements. The city, for instance, is credited with inventing the American cocktail. It was a Frenchman who made up a concoction of brandy and bitters in a coquetier (egg cup) – hence cocktail. Among the best known New Orleans alcoholic creations are Ramos Gin Fizz, a smooth mixture of cream, gin and orange flower water; Sazerac, a blend of rye whisky and bitters, and the Hurricane which is poured into a 29 ounce hand-blown crested glass at Pat O'Briens, a famous bar in St Peter Street. It claims to be the busiest bar in the world.

A large-scale example of *lagniappe* is the Mardi Gras festival. A series of fancy dress parades, street parties and grand balls culminates on Shrove Tuesday every year in the biggest bean-feast in the States. Mardi Gras means Fat Tuesday, and Fat is a jazz idiomatic term for over-indulgence. (A new modern city complex of plush shops and apartment houses is called Fat City). The first carnival day parade was held in 1857 when masked riders on horseback and crinolined ladies in open carriages tossed fruit and sweets to the crowds. Today the crowds are showered with medallions, beads and trinkets specially made for the occasion. All the festivities are organised by 'mystick krewes' – elite societies made up of influential residents who provide financial support and ensure that the traditions of the carnival are maintained. On Mardi Gras visitors from all over the world come to watch the parades and the ornately decorated floats, a spectacle only rivalled by the carnival in Rio de Janeiro.

Although New Orleans hopes to have more than 36,000 hotel rooms by the mid-eighties, the chance of finding one during Mardi Gras time is slim, unless it has been booked well in advance.

Another difficult time to find accommodation is during important American football matches in New Orleans. These fixtures are held in the Superdome – a gigantic arena which claims to be the 'world's largest steel-constructed hall unobstructed by posts'. The top of the dome is 273 feet high, ballooning like an airship at anchor above the skyline. Joggers use the circumference to run a measured mile!

On a good day, it can hold more than 95,000 people, but if they don't all turn up, adjustable stands give the place a more cosy appearance. Also, the cleverly-striped upholstery on the seats gives the impression

The Festivals

Here is a rough guide to the most exciting and colourful festivals held in New Orleans. Every season is marked by a celebration, although the actual dates vary from year to year. Whatever time of year you visit, however, somewhere in the city there is likely to be a festival in progress.

JANUARY 6TH TO FEBRUARY OR MARCH: The processions and parades of the greatest carnival of all, the Mardi Gras, which culminates on Mardi Gras itself, the Tuesday before Lent.

MID MARCH: Parades celebrate St Patrick's Day in the two main New Orleans' parishes.

MID APRIL: The time for the Crawfish Festival in St Bernard Parish, which coincides with the height of the crawfish (crayfish) season. Plenty of chances to try this favourite New Orleans delicacy.

LATE APRIL TO EARLY MAY: Two weekends are entirely devoted to the Jazz and Heritage Festival, when over 1,000 musicians perform and Louisiana demonstrates its crafts and cooking in the Fairground.

Also this is the season for the Spring Fiesta, when the private homes in the French Quarter and Garden District are opened to the public, and the hosts dress in 18th- and 19-th century costumes, Candlelight parades and tours of plantation houses are also included on the agenda.

LATE JUNE TO EARLY JULY: Louisiana's culinary delights are displayed in food-tasting booths during the Food Festival.

MID JULY: The Louisiana Oyster Festival is an excuse to gorge on this delicious shellfish at Galliano, in Lafourche Parish.

LATE JULY: The International Tarpon Rodeo is held at Grand Isle, in Jefferson Parish.

EARLY AUGUST: Jefferson Seafood Festival. More opportunities to try local delicacies.

MID AUGUST: At Grand Isle, Jefferson Parish, the fishing fleet is involved in the colourful Blessing of the Fleet.

LATE AUGUST: Jefferson Redfish Rodeo.

EARLY OCTOBER– Gumbo, a soup usually based on a mixture of chicken and fish, a New Orleans speciality, is the object of the Gumbo Festival in Jefferson Parish.

Also at this time the Spanish Heritage and Cultural Festival is held at Chalmette in St Bernard Parish

LATE OCTOBER: Bouillabaisse Festival, at Larose in Lafourche Parish.

MID NOVEMBER: An opportunity to examine the crafts of Louisiana is given at the Crafts Festival in St Tammany Parish.

EARLY DECEMBER: Louisiana Orange Festival, at Burns in Plaquemine Parish.

to those watching events on the television that there is a full house.

Even when it is half empty, the Superdome after a match can bring chaos to the city's traffic.

The only remaining streetcar line still operating in New Orleans (it runs through St Charles Avenue in the Garden District) claims to be the oldest continuously operating street railway in the world. Introduced in 1835 as a horse-drawn street railway, it was later powered by steam. When the overhead electrification was completed at the turn of the century, the system covered over 225 miles of New Orleans streets. Now buses have taken over on most of the routes – even on Desire Parkway, which inspired Tennessee Williams to write the play *A Streetcar Named Desire*.

Another famous writer, Frances Parkinson Keyes, lived at Beauregard House at 1114 Chartres Street, to the east of the city. Built in 1826, it was the residence of the Confederate General after whom it was named. It is open to the public, as is Gallier Hall at 524 St Charles Avenue, once New Orleans City Hall, and now a 'stately home' filled with paintings and exquisite antiques.

To leave the city by car, the choice of route south is limited to two bridges over the Mississippi. The Huey P Long bridge (see page 14) is named after the former governor of Louisiana who was assassinated in 1935; and the Greater New Orleans Bridge carries the Pontchartrain Expressway to the south bank of the river and to the suburbs of Terry Town, Gretna and Algiers.

Five miles to the north of the city, the longest highway bridge over water in the world crosses the 23-mile wide Lake Pontchartrain. The causeway carries a four-lane divided highway which bisects 610 square miles of the lake just a few feet off the surface of the water, giving traffic a kind of switchback ride from time to time to allow river traffic to pass underneath at several points. An eight-mile stretch is sometimes totally out of sight of land. When the second span was completed in 1969, the bridge had cost over £20 million to put up. It opened up the route for thousands of motorists into the lush Louisiana countryside, with its magnificent antebellum houses and multifarious attractions.

▲ *Jubilant crowds throng the streets during Mardi Gras, a festival as old as the city itself*

▶ *Two of New Orleans' most notorious residents, the pirates Pierre and Jean Lafitte, are said to have used this blacksmith's shop as a disguise for their smuggling activities*

◀ *Riding the old St Charles streetcar, seen here in Canal Street, is one of the most enjoyable ways of touring New Orleans*

New Orleans Directory

PROVINCIAL MOTOR HOTEL: 1024 Chartres St, tel 581 4995. 100 rooms. Family-run, French Quarter establishment with pool and saunas. Moderate.

ROYAL ORLEANS HOTEL: 621 St Louis St, tel 529 5333. 386 rooms. French Quarter hotel with pay valet garage, pool and restaurants. Expensive.

SAINT LOUIS: 730 Bienville St, tel 581 7300. 66 rooms. French Quarter hotel featuring suites, cocktail lounge and pay garage. Expensive.

SHERATON INN – INTERNATIONAL AIRPORT: 2150 Veterans' Blvd, tel 467 3111, freephone 800 325 3535. 253 rooms. Restaurant, swimming pool and sauna. Transport to and from airport. Moderate.

TRAVELODGE AT DOWNTOWN NEW ORLEANS: 1630 Canal St, tel 586 0110. 216 rooms. Handily placed for the Superdome, with pool and rooftop meeting rooms. Moderate.

VIEUX CARRÉ MOTOR LODGE: 920 N Rampart St, tel 524 0461. 100 rooms. Friendly hotel in the French Quarter, with small pool, restaurant and courtyard. Inexpensive.

WARWICK HOTEL: 1315 Gravier St, tel 586 0100. 176 rooms. Located near the French Quarter and the Superdome. Facilities include free parking, saunas and a cocktail lounge. Moderate.

RESTAURANTS

Listed here are a few of New Orleans' many fine restaurants, chosen either because they are recommended by the American Automobile Association, or because of their particular appeal. They are classified, as a rough guide to cost, as either expensive, moderate or inexpensive. Many of New Orleans' more expensive restaurants, it should be noted, insist on a strict dress code; men are expected to wear a jacket and tie.

THE ANDREW JACKSON: 221 Royal St, tel 529 2603. Fine restaurant opened in the mid-sixties by the Sevin Brothers. Its tasteful décor includes a

life-sized sculpture of Andrew Jackson. Of the house specialities, veal King Ferdinand VII and Chateaubriand steak are highly recommended. Expensive.

ANTOINE'S: 713 St Louis St, tel 581 4422. Long-established 19th-century family restaurant with a totally French menu. Many acclaimed house specials and a fine wine cellar. Expensive.

ARNAVO'S: 813 Rue Bienville, tel 523 5433. This restaurant was founded in 1918 by Count Arnaud Cazenave, and the menu still features some of his specialities, such as shrimp Arnaud and oysters Bienville. Moderate.

BENIHANA OF TOKYO: 720 St Louis St, tel 522 0425. Japanese restaurant that makes a welcome change in the French Quarter. All food prepared at communal *hibachi* tables. Expensive.

THE BON TON: 401 Magazine St, tel 524 3386. Specialities of this Creole eaterie are seafood and old Cajun family recipes. A popular place at lunchtimes, but is closed at weekends. Moderate.

BRENNAN'S: 417 Royal St, tel 525 9711. A converted 19th-century house boasting no less than ten dining rooms. The mainly seafood menu features quail and crabs. Expensive.

H C BRUNING: 1870 Orpheum Av, tel 282 9395. Lakeside restaurant with massive mahogany bar. Simple seafood at sensible prices. Inexpensive.

COMMANDER'S PALACE: Washington Av and Coliseum St, tel 899 8221. A family restaurant situated in the Garden District, specialising in Creole dishes. Live jazz during weekend mornings. Moderate.

CORINNE DUNBAR'S: 1617 St Charles Av, tel 525 2957. Daily-changing variety of food à la Creole. Closed Sundays. Moderate.

FELIX'S: 739 Iberville St, tel 522 0324/4440. Steaks and seafood are the featured dishes at this French Quarter restaurant. Moderate.

GALATOIRE'S RESTURANT: 209 Bourbon St, tel 525 2021. Family-run establishment with the emphasis on Creole-French cuisine. Specialities include trout Marquery and

shrimp remoulade. Superb coffee. Inexpensive.

KOLBS RESTAURANT: 125 St Charles St, tel 522 8278. Good food served in an atmosphere of days gone by. Children's menu. Inexpensive.

LA BOUCHERIE/GUMBO POT: 330 Chartres St, tel 522 6672. Eaterie offering Creole and Cajun dishes, plus salads and toasted sandwiches. A disco and games room is above. Inexpensive.

LE RUTH'S: 636 Franklin St, Gretna, tel 372 4914. High-class French cuisine for which the owner, Warren LeRuth, has won many prizes. Variety of local seafood and an extensive wine list. Well worth the 15-minute drive from downtown New Orleans. Expensive.

MAISON PIERRE: 430 Dauphine St, tel 529 5521. Fine French served in attractive dining-room. A strict dress code applies. Expensive.

MASSON'S RESTAURANT FRANÇAIS: 7200 Pontchartrain Blvd, tel 283 2525. Predominantly French food served in a relaxed atmosphere. Children's menu. Nearby is a yacht harbour. Moderate.

THE OLD SPAGHETTI FACTORY: 330 St Charles Av, tel 561 1068. As its name implies, this eaterie serves a plethora of pasta. Notably unusual décor, with odd antiques such as a preacher's pulpit and an old tramcar. Inexpensive.

ORIGINAL PAPA JOE'S CAFE: 600 Bourbon St, tel 529 5576. A French Quarter café providing nightly live entertainment. Traditional New Orleans drinks are served with the various steaks and seafood. Inexpensive.

T PITTARI'S: 4200 S Claiborne Av, tel 891 2801. This restaurant, first opened in 1895, is famous for its 'Montana wild game skillet (a buffalo, venison and elk mixture). Seafood dominates the menu. Moderate.

PONTCHARTRAIN HOTEL – CARIBBEAN ROOM: 2031 St Charles Av, tel 524 0581. Luxury restaurant housed in a top-class hotel. Mainly seafood menu. Expensive.

RUTH'S CHRIS STEAK HOUSE: 3633 Veterans' Blvd, tel 888 3600. Variety of steaks served with generous side-salads. Moderate.

TCHOUPITOULAS PLANTATION RESTAURANT: 6535 River Rd, Westbank in Avondale, tel 436 1277. Leisurely dining in a delightful old country atmosphere. The restaurant is set in 12-acre wooded grounds, 30 minutes drive from downtown New Orleans. The special 'Jezebel' cocktail should start off a devilishly good meal. Moderate.

TORTORICI'S: 441 Royal St, tel 522 4295. A French Quarter restaurant featuring both Italian and American dishes. Children's menu. Closed Sundays. Moderate.

THE VIEUX CARRÉ RESTAURANT: 241 Bourbon St, tel 524 0114. Fine French and Creole cuisine served in one of the French Quarter's oldest dining-rooms (built 1831). Moderate.

TRANSPORT

MOISANT INTERNATIONAL AIRPORT: 12 miles W of New Orleans at Kenner. Over a dozen major domestic and foreign airlines operate in and out of Moisant. It is the main transfer terminal for Mexico and the South American subcontinent.

TAXIS: Cabs are easily hailed in both the downtown area and the French Quarter. Elsewhere it is best to telephone. Major companies are: Checker, tel 943 2411; Ed's, tel 522 0241; United, tel 522 9771; Yellow, tel 525 3311.

BUSES: Cheap and frequent bus services operate within the city limits. For further information contact the New Orleans Transit Office, tel 586 2192. The last remaining streetcar line is along St Charles Av.

TRAINS: The Union Passenger Terminal is the main railway station and is located at 1001 Loyola Av. For train times and information contact AMTRAK National Information Center, tel free phone 800 874 2800.

CAR HIRE: There are several car rental firms operating in New Orleans, their rates varying according to car size but insurance is usually included in the price. Major

companies are: Airways, tel 466 9321; Avis, tel 523 4317; Budget, tel 525 9417; Hertz, tel 568 1645.

TOURING INFORMATION

SIGHTSEEING: Mississippi riverboat trips leave from Toulouse St Wharf and Canal St Docks, while on dry land Peggy Wilson's Guided Trolley Tour is an interesting excursion, tel 895 0412 or 866 1689.

AAA: The association has a motorists' inquiry office at 3445 N Causeway Blvd, Metairie, tel 837 1080.

VISITOR INFORMATION CENTER: 344 Royal St, tel 522 8772 (for cultural events 522 2787). Guides and brochures on all the city's attractions and events.

NEWSPAPERS: The *Figaro* and *Gris Gris* journals highlight all French Quarter entertainment.

SHOPPING

FRENCH QUARTER: An exotic district offering the tourist many and varied opportunities for shopping. The majority of the shops are in Royal, Chartres and St Ann Sts. Goods range from antiques, gifts and Creole food through to handicraft, clothes and shoes. A colourful French market is down by the Mississippi, while a short distance away in Decatur St is the Flea Market with its collection of jewellery, pottery and knick-knacks.

RIVERBEND: Carrollton Av. A small region of Victorian shops alongside the Mississippi dealing mainly in gifts and luxury goods. Pleasant restaurants nearby.

UPTOWN SQUARE: off Broadway and Perrier. Modern shopping precinct built around courtyards and plazas.

FAT CITY: N Causeway, Veterans' Blvd, Division St

and W Esplanade. Large downtown shopping area.

DEPARTMENT STORES: All are central and within reach of the French Quarter. The main old-established stores being Godchaux, 828 Canal St; D H Holmes Company, 819 Canal St; Maison Blanche, 901 Canal St.

DESTREHAM: Destreham Plantation House, some ten miles past the airport on River Rd, offers a change from conventional shopping. Here the tourist can combine looking round a historic home with buying the odd gift or antique.

MUSEUMS

THE CABILDO: Jackson Sq, tel 522 8832. Historic building with a chequered past, now housing local culture and trade exhibits. Also features Napoleon's death mask.

CABRINI DOLL MUSEUM: 1218 Burgundy St, tel 586 5204. Impressive collection of international dolls. Children's books and art are also featured.

HISTORIC NEW ORLEANS COLLECTION: 533 Royal St, tel 523 7146. One of the few buildings which escaped the French Quarter fire of 1794. Contains a vast collection of historic Louisiana art and documents.

HISTORICAL PHARMACY MUSEUM: 514 Chartres St. A former drug-store, built in the 1820s, now houses a series of exhibits depicting the development of early medicine. Also Voodoo exhibits.

LOUISIANA WILDLIFE MUSEUM: 400 Royal St. Native mammals and reptiles plus various bird specimens.

MUSEE CONTI WAX MUSEUM: 917 Conti St, tel 525 2605. Various tableaux, featuring fine costumary, illustrate both the historical and somewhat mysterious past of New Orleans and Louisiana.

NEW ORLEANS MUSEUM OF ART: Lelong Av, City Park, tel 488 2631. A neo-classical building housing a permanent collection of international

exhibits depicting the development of art. Temporary major exhibitions take place occasionally. Free entry on Thursdays.

PRESBYTERE: Jackson Sq, tel 581 4321. An early 19th-century building originally intended to be a courthouse. Now, owned by the Louisiana State Museum, it houses displays of costumes, toys, art and jewellery. Also exhibited is an 1861 submarine.

SUN OAK: FAUBOURG MARIGNY COLLECTION: 2020 Burgundy St, tel 945 0322. The two buildings are restored Creole cottages dating back to the mid-19th century. Set amid lovely gardens, the houses contain fine French, Creole and Acadian antiques. Opening is restricted and usually by appointment only.

VOODOO MUSEUM: 739 Bourbon St, tel 523 2906. The only museum of its type in America. The history of this weird cult is charted with ritual objects such as drums, grisgris and even a Voodoo altar. Psychic readings and gift shop.

PLACES TO SEE

BEAUREGARD HOUSE: 1113 Chartres St, tel 523 7257. Originally the 19th-century home of a wealthy New Orleans auctioneer, then of General Beauregard, a Civil War leader. Later, the writer Frances Parkinson Keyes lived here. It is a fine example of a Creole home with a notable twin staircase.

CASA HOVE: 723 Toulouse St, tel 525 7827. One of the oldest buildings in the Mississippi valley, dating back to the 1720s. Superb example of early Spanish architecture. There is a parfumerie on the ground floor, but the upper house may be viewed.

CHALMETTE NATIONAL HISTORICAL PARK: Arabi, tel 271 2412. Site of the 1815 Battle of New Orleans, where a hastily assembled army led by General Jackson defeated the British. Original cannons and ramparts still in situ.

GALLIER HOUSE: 1118–1132 Royal St. The 19th-century

home of an eminent architect. The house is fully restored with period furniture.

HERMAN-GRIMA HOUSE: 820 St Louis St, tel 525 5661. Built in 1831, this 3-storey mansion is surrounded by courtyards and stables (now converted to a shop). Its antique collection is still being added to.

INTERNATIONAL TRADE MART: 2 Canal St. Known as the 'Buying Crossroads of the Hemisphere', this is the hub of New Orleans' maritime industry. Two floors are open to the public. On the 31st storey is the Louisiana Maritime Museum which charts every aspect of local shipping history. An observation deck affording fine views of the city and docks is on the same floor. A revolving cocktail bar called 'Top of the Mart' and offering nightly entertainment is on the 33rd floor.

LAKE PONTCHARTRAIN CAUSEWAY: N of Causeway Blvd. At 24 miles long, the longest overwater roadway bridge in the world. The 4-lane highway has three overpasses and two opening spans to allow marine traffic through. It was completed in 1956 at a cost of $51 million.

LOOM ROOM: 623 Royal St, tel 522 7101. A chance to see local weavers at work. Many examples on display.

MADAME JOHN'S LEGACY: 632 Dumaine St, tel 581 4321. A Creole planter's house furnished with many early antiques. Although claimed to be the oldest building on the Mississippi, it was probably not built until 1789 – following the great fire.

OLD URSULINE CONVENT: 1114 Chartres St. The first nunnery established in New Orleans. Sisters at that time were the only teachers and nurses, and founded the first schools and an orphanage. After 1824 the building became the state's legal HQ. The lovely courtyard is reached via an unusual gateway.

RIVERGATE EXHIBITION CENTER: 4 Canal St. Large modern building where major trade fairs and the annual Mardi Gras take place.

ST LOUIS CATHEDRAL: Jackson Sq. Built in 1794 and controversially remodelled in 1851 from the original Spanish style to Greek Revival. The basilica remains a popular place of worship.

US CUSTOMS HOUSE: Decatur and Canal Sts. Built in 1849 on the site of the old Fort St Louis.

WASHINGTON ARTILLERY PARK: Off Jackson Sq. Large park with fountains, gardens, a playground and views of the French Quarter.

SPORT

SUPERDOME: Poydras St, tel 587 3663. At 680ft, the building's diameter is reputedly the largest in the world. American football, basketball and baseball are all played in this totally windowless, circular sports centre. There is seating for 95,000 spectators and the air-conditioning is computer-controlled. The building is also the venue for large-scale musical and theatrical productions. Guided tours.

HORSE-RACING: New Orleans has two race-tracks. Fair Grounds, off Gentilly Blvd, from November to March and Jefferson Downs, near Lake Pontchartrain, from April to September.

FISHING: The bayous (creeks) of Louisiana offer excellent fishing. For fishing trips and tackle hire, tel 522 8772.

CHILDREN'S RECREATION: tel 586 4461 for various playground events in the city.

NIGHTLIFE

AL HIRT'S: 501 Bourbon St, tel 525 6167. Trumpet virtuoso Al Hirt and his band are the resident jazzmen here, plus guest visits by other top-flight groups.

BLUE ROOM: Fairmont Hotel, University Pla, tel 529 7111. Top entertainment and fine Creole food in sumptuous surroundings.

DUKE'S PLACE: Monteleone Hotel, 214 Royal St, tel 581 1567. Good old Dixieland jazz is the order of the day at this

rooftop venue. Superb views of the French Quarter and the Mississippi.

809 CLUB: 809 St Louis St. Top-class floor shows and revues. Occasionally female impersonators.

THE NATCHEZ: Toulouse St Wharf, tel 586 8777. An evening out with a difference. A dinner cruise on an old-style riverboat. Does not operate Mondays.

OLD ABSINTHE HOUSE: 400 Bourbon St. The original bar was at 240 Bourbon St but all fixtures and fittings were moved during the Prohibition era. Live music is rhythm-and-blues or progressive jazz.

PADDOCK BAR AND LOUNGE: 309 Bourbon St. More good jazz here. Much frequented by the racing set, as the memento-clad walls will testify.

PAT O'BRIENS: 718 Peter St, tel 525 4823. Internationally famous bar with rousing piano entertainment. The building is split into a patio, main bar and lounge. *The* drink here is the tall red concoction called 'The Hurricane'.

LE PETIT THEATRE DU VIEUX CARRÉ: 616 St Peter St, tel 522 2081. Very old non-professional theatre in the heart of the French Quarter. The high acting standard makes it well worth a visit.

PRESERVATION HALL: 726 St Peter St, tel 522 2081. A treat for the fans of purist, New Orleans jazz. Many of the musicians have played here for decades. The few basic wooden chairs and benches help to keep the old-style atmosphere.

TULANE UNIVERSITY THEATRE: Phoenix Theatre, 9 McAlister Dr (Tulane Campus), tel 865 6204. A college theatre staging high-standard productions.

CLIMATE

New Orleans has a sub-tropical climate, with average daily summer temperatures of 90 This drops ro around 45 in winter. Humidity averages 63% annually, while rainfall amounts to 54 inches per year.

The Golden West
– Southern California

Drifters and dreamers, the ambitious and the pleasure-seeking converge on southern California, a land of great natural beauty, climatic extremes and extraordinary diversity.

In this part of California stands the highest point in the USA outside Alaska – Mount Whitney in the Sequoia National Park. Yet only 80 miles away Death Valley, which sinks to 282 feet below sea level, is the lowest point in the country, and in summer one of the hottest.

Man has made his own contributions to California's variety. Near Monterey, where

Steinbeck set his classic novel *Cannery Row*, is Carmel, a beautiful forest village encircled by mountains and rolling hills, where, among the narrow streets and old houses, the 20th century is left behind.

In total contrast, away from the magnificent coastline, is Palm Springs in the Colorado Desert. This is the playground of the super-rich, where life revolves around golf, tennis and 6,500 swimming pools beneath a sun which shines 350 days a year.

Palm-fringed beaches, on the other hand, are an attraction to all along the coast north and south of Los Angeles, one of America's greatest and most glamorous cities, dominated in the public mind by Hollywood, its star-studded suburb.

There is also Disneyland, the most magical of man-made kingdoms, where young and old can lose themselves for a while in an escapist's paradise.

Yet wherever you go in southern California, there is always the influence of those first Spanish missions of the 18th century, in the place names, the architecture, and the people.

A golden Californian sunset over the beach at Pacific Palisades, a short distance from Los Angeles

ONE INCH—APPROX 156 MILES

31

Stretching from Mexico, south of San Diego, to Oregon, north of Crescent City, 1,000 miles of America's western seaboard belongs to California. Most of its 21.5 million people crowd the cities and towns along the Pacific coastline. California is not only the most populated state; it is also the third largest after Alaska and oil-rich Texas.

Lured by sunshine, sparkling surf and golden sands, the millions came convinced that they would find in California a new kind of paradise on earth.

Yet only 140 years ago, only about 700 Americans were known to live in the 158,000 square miles of land between the Sierra Nevada and the Pacific Ocean. They, too, came to look for paradise, thinking it was to be found in the golden seams of the soil. As more and more prospectors arrived, the famous 'Forty-niners' of the frenetic gold rush of 1849 really believed that they had found their El Dorado, and that all their wildest dreams of untold riches were waiting only to be sifted from the dust under their feet.

For a decade, the cry of Eureka (Greek for 'I have found it!') echoed through the gold country around Placerville to the north-east of San Francisco. The state has adopted the cry as its motto, even though there is little gold now to be found, and certainly none for the casual prospector. But 50 years after the gold rush ended, Californians founded another kind of El Dorado in the southern part of the state. They called it Hollywood.

To the rest of the world, the film industry

that grew up there represented everything that was noble, successful and desirable. Fame brought undreamt-of rewards to these new kind of prospectors.

Against the backdrop of blue Pacific rollers, glistening brown tanned bodies on white sands and luxury beyond measure, the idols of millions throughout the world were created in the dream factories of Hollywood.

But southern California is no longer the mecca of only the world's beautiful people. The harsh economic realities have put paid to the dreams. Los Angeles no longer even encourages such a romantic vision of its sprawling suburb. Instead, like much of southern California, it has attracted the industrial entrepreneurs.

Profits from steel and aluminium for the massive aircraft industry on the door-step of Los Angeles and San Diego, and oil and gas plants in the vicinity of Los Angeles and Long Beach far exceed the wealth produced by gold in its hey-day or by the film industry when at its peak.

California is also America's leading agricultural state. Southern California has a Mediterranean climate while in the northern half of the state the prevailing west winds tend to bring more rain. This variety of climate provides California with a rich harvest of food products; it grows the most prolific range of crops – everything except tobacco. When the navel orange was introduced in 1873 it was the beginning of a flourishing citrus-fruit-growing industry, and grapes, which grow in abundance, are

A Joshua Tree in the Mohave Desert. This rare species of the lily family grows to 30 to 40 feet high, and can be as much as 300 years old. They provide valuable shelter for desert wildlife, such as lizards and birds

now turned into wine that has a growing reputation throughout the world. Nearly everything grows well in southern California. Yucca, (lily-like plants), cacti and other desert plants and the ubiquitous palm stand shoulder to shoulder with the eucalyptus and the live oak. Climatic extremes exist too, producing such contrasts as lofty, ice-bound mountains which can match the Swiss Alps in size and grandeur, the world's tallest trees, and deserts as hot and dry as the Sahara in North Africa.

Southern California betrays its Spanish connections. The names of many familiar places bear witness to the years of Spanish colonisation. Through its early domination of Mexico, Spain imposed a language and culture on California long before the first American trappers and fur traders ventured across the mountains from the east, or the sailors took their first tentative steps across the beaches. Indian tribes – over 100,000 strong before the first white man set foot on Californian soil – between them shared a score of different languages, with some 135 regional dialects. Disease brought by the Spaniards decimated their numbers and during the Gold Rush they were virtually obliterated by the avarice and belligerence of the American prospectors. It was a Portuguese navigator in the service of the

Spanish Crown, Juan Rodriguez Cabrillo, who in 1542 made the first European discovery of the California coast. He landed near San Diego, where a national monument overlooks the spot where he is believed to have come ashore.

Thirty-seven years later, Sir Francis Drake paused in his pursuit of Spanish treasure ships to drop anchor 30 miles north-west of San Francisco at what is now called Drake's Bay, and named the territory New Albion on behalf of Elizabeth I. But it was Spain's Sebastian Vizcaino who, in 1602, imposed lasting Spanish influence on the coastal settlements. More than 160 years went by before King Charles of Spain took a serious interest in the prospect of making California a colony. Marching north from Mexico, Gaspar de Portola led an expedition to San Diego and made it southern California's first permanent settlement. In 1781 Los Angeles was the second pueblo (or town) to be established. With the Army came the Church. California's 21 religious settlements by 1823 extended 600 miles from San Diego to Sonoma, north of San Francisco, and most have been carefully preserved. Moving slowly north, the grey-robed Franciscans built each settlement a day's travel apart.

When Mexico became independent of Spain in 1822, California for a time moved closer to her southern neighbour.

The 19th century, too, made California feel uneasy over the United States' territorial ambitions and there was growing discontent over Mexico's influence. In the end the dissent grew into open revolt, and when Mexico finally decided to re-impose its authority, California endured the one and only military battle to be fought on its soil. The encounter took place in December 1846 at San Pasqual, to the north-east of San Diego, at the cost of 22 lives.

Fourteen months later, after hostilities had ended, California officially became part of the United States in February 1848. Full statehood had to wait until 1850. By that time California had already attracted 90,000 settlers. Many of them arrived during the Gold Rush. They came by boat round Cape Horn, by boat and road across Panama, or they made epic journeys in covered wagons across the plains, mountains and deserts of central America. The railroad track, too, forged ahead both east and west; by 1867 the west was linked by rail with the central and eastern states.

California's most significant population explosion, however, came at the beginning of this century, when the motor car suddenly made travel to the western outposts of the continent a less foolhardy adventure than it had been. Californians took to the motor car with enthusiasm and characteristic aplomb. The result of this moving love affair has been to make the state more dependent on its road network than most others in America. Los Angeles is totally dominated by its freeways, and California has on the whole kept its thousands of miles of excellently maintained highways free of tolls. Ironically, on the most famous scenic route, the 17-mile drive between Pacific Grove and Carmel, payment is required. The route takes in stunning scenery, including a bird's-eye view of Monterey from Shepherd's Knoll where, on a clear day, you can see the Santa Cruz mountains 35 miles to the north. At Carberry Knoll, sweeping vistas open up of Carmel Bay and the Santa Lucia mountains. Point Joe was where several ships came to grief on stormy nights when mariners thought they were entering Monterey Bay.

Look out for the Restless Sea along this route – the name given to an area of unusual

The rocky Pacific coast near the old town of Monterey, a green and lush stretch of California's seaboard which is a haven for seabirds and wild flowers

turbulence which results from the uneven contours of the ocean floor. Seals, birds, cormorants and gulls congregate at Seal Rock, and further on at Cypress Point, there are spectacular views of the coast, including another coastal wonder 20 miles to the south – Big Sur.

Big Sur is a region of cliffs and jagged rocks pounded by the sea, a kaleidoscope of colours and shapes created by the awesome display of nature. Man's contribution is the Pfeiffer Big Sur State Park off State Route 1. It covers 821 acres, and has facilities for camping, picknicking, hiking, fishing, swimming, and riding.

Monterey, with a population of 27,000, was California's capital under Spanish, Mexican and American rule. This is where John Steinbeck's famous novel, *Cannery Row*, was set. Most of the fish canneries that flourished over half a century ago have gone, but in their place tourist restaurants, art galleries and handicraft shops have brought a more leisurely mood to the area. A lot happens in Monterey. It is the focus of the Monterey Peninsula where, apart from the start of the 17-mile drive, tourists can enjoy magnificent golf courses and other all-year-round entertainment facilities. The Monterey State Historic Park in

---

MONTEREY

Hotels

CYPRESS GARDENS MOTEL: 1150 Munras Av, tel 373 2761. 45 rooms. Moderate.

DOUBLETREE INN OF MONTEREY: 2 Portola Plaza, tel 649 4511. 375 rooms. Expensive.

MONTERO LODGE: 1240 Munras Av, tel 375 6002. 20 rooms. Inexpensive-moderate.

RANCHO MONTEREY MOTEL: 1200 Munras Av, tel 372 5821. 27 rooms. Moderate-expensive.

Restaurants

THE CLOCK GARDEN RESTAURANT: 565 Abrego St, in Old Monterey, tel 375 6100. Intimate and charming, with a varied menu. Moderate.

LOU'S FISH GROTTO: 50 Fisherman's Wharf, tel 372 3655. Splendid location overlooking harbour. Unpretentious family restaurant specialising in good seafood. Moderate.

WILLIE LUM'S CHINA ROW: 444 Cannery Row, tel 373 8494. Chinese, Polynesian and American cuisine. Dining room overlooks Monterey Bay. Moderate-expensive.

Places of Interest

ALLEN KNIGHT MARITIME MUSUEM. 550 Calle Principal. Portrays the sailing ship era and the fishing and whaling history of Monterey through exhibits, pictures and models.

MONTEREY STATE HISTORIC PARK: 210 Olivier St. 7-acre site which preserves the history and architecture of old Monterey.

SOUTHERN CALIFORNIA

CARMEL

Hotels

COACHMAN'S INN: 1 blk S San Carlos at 7th Av, tel 624 6421. 29 rooms. Moderate-expensive.

JADE TREE INN: 1 blk N Junipero St between 5th and 6th Avs, tel 624 1831. 55 rooms. Moderate-expensive.

PINE INN: Ocean Av between Lincoln and Monte Verdi, tel 624 3851. Expensive.

Restaurants

FISH HOUSE ON THE PARK: 6th and Junipero Av, tel 624 1766. Opposite the park, this restaurant specialises in locally caught and imported seafood delicacies. Expensive.

MARQUIS RESTAURANT: 3 blks N off Ocean Av, at Dolphin Inn, 4th Av and San Carlos, tel 624 8068. Moderate-expensive.

Places of Interest

MISSION SAN CARLOS BORROMEO DEL RÍO CARMELO: 3080 Rio Rd. Church established by Father Serra in 1770. He is buried in front of the altar.

POINT LOBOS STATE RESERVE: 1,276 acres of rugged seacoast where you can find Monterey Cypress, wild flowers and sea lions.

The height of opulence – the Neptune Pool at Hearst Castle. The pool is lit at night by light filtered through alabaster globes to give the illusion of moonlight

Olivier Street also catches the atmosphere of Old Monterey and marks the site of an early attempt by a Spanish expedition, led by Sebastian Vizcaino, to land at Monterey Bay. They abandoned the effort without realising the significance of their landfall.

The city maintains California's first theatre to charge admission. An English sailor of Scottish ancestry, called Jack Swan, built a house at Pacific and Scott Streets, and in 1846 opened it as a lodging house for sailors. Later it was turned into a playhouse, and now it gives special evening performances. The theatre also has a collection of relics of early California on show.

One of the most famous 18th-century missions is to be found at Carmel. It was originally established by Father Junipero Serra at Monterey in 1770, and moved to Carmel's Rio Road the next year. Some of Serra's books and documents recalling the mission's early days can be inspected together with other historical items.

About 80 miles south stands one of the world's most flamboyant edifices – Hearst's Castle. William Randolph Hearst was America's wealthiest newspaper and magazine tycoon. He started to build the main house in 1922, on 123 acres atop a 1,600-foot mountain called the Enchanted Hill, overlooking the Pacific, five miles from San Simeon along a twisting, winding road. But he never saw it finished. It is 137-foot high, and contains over 100 rooms; 38 bedrooms, 38 bathrooms, 14 sitting rooms, a film theatre, two libraries and several other reception and dining rooms.

Seven years after he died in 1951, aged 88, the Hispano-Moorish mansion he called La Casa Grande, with its 50 million dollar collection of art treasures and antiques, was presented to the state. More than 6 million visitors have toured the estate since: there are three two-hour tours, one through the gardens, terraces, pools and houses of the grounds, and the second and third visit various sections of the main mansion. In the grounds are two swimming pools. The open-air Neptune Pool, constructed of concrete and marble and 104 feet long, holds 345,000 gallons of water. Its main feature is a series of white marble statues in recessed alcoves which look as though they are floating on the surface of the water. A 200,000-gallon Roman indoor pool is so large it accommodates two tennis courts on its roof, and is lined with brilliantly coloured Venetian and glass tiles. Hearst even imported all kinds of wildlife, which still roam freely on the hills of the estate.

Among attractions nearer Los Angeles are several lesser known delights. In Arcadia, for instance – a city of 47,000 people to the north-west of downtown Los Angeles – the Santa Anita Park in West Huntington Drive has one of America's most prominent thoroughbred horse-racing tracks, where the familiar starting gate, the photo finish, the electrical timer and the totalizator were first developed. About 20 miles to the west, Riverside – another Los Angeles suburb

RIVERSIDE

Hotels

AMERICAN MOTELODGE: 1350 University Av, tel 682 1144. 80 rooms. Moderate-expensive.

BEST WESTERN SAGE AND SAND MOTEL: 1971 University Av, tel 684 6363. 45 rooms. Moderate.

RAMADA INN: 1150 University Av, tel 682 2771. 100 rooms. Expensive.

Restaurants

PITRUZZELO'S CONTINENTAL CUISINE: 287 La Cadena Dr, tel 686 6787. Italian food, steaks and seafood. Also an extensive wine list. Moderate.

REUBEN'S: 3640 Central Av, tel 683 3842. Early Californian décor. Children's menu. Moderate-expensive.

Places of Interest

MISSION INN: 3649 7th St. A mission-style hotel having Spanish antiques, paintings, and other relics of the early Spanish missions. St Francis Chapel has a 200-year-old altar and Tiffany windows. Adjacent is the International Shrine of Aviators, where mementoes of famous flyers are kept.

MOUNT RUBIDOUX: This 1,337-foot-high mountain rises above the Santa Ana River at the W edge of the city. On the summit are the Father Serra Cross and the World Peace Tower.

ARCADIA

Hotel

BEST WESTERN WESTERNER INN: 161 Colorado Pl, tel 447 3501. 76 rooms. Expensive.

Restaurants

ROYAL TURTLE RESTAURANT: 325 E Live Oak, tel 446 5201. Attractive restaurant with a large selection of dishes available. Children's menu. Moderate-expensive.

SAW MILL RESTAURANT: 57 Wheeler Av at 1st St, tel 446 4488. Steaks and seafoods. Moderate-expensive.

Places of Interest

LOS ANGELES STATE AND COUNTY ARBORETUM: 301 N Baldwin Av. Horticultural research centre with 127 acres of trees and shrubs, hot houses, a bird sanctuary and a reference library.

great collections of rare books and manuscripts is housed. It was left by millionaire transport industrialist Henry Edward Huntington, who built up his library and art collection from 1914 until his death in 1927. This house, in Oxford Road, has seven main galleries and 15 smaller galleries containing paintings, drawing, tapestries and silver. There are two extensive collections of clocks and miniatures produced in England and France in the 18th century. More than 200,000 volumes are contained in the rare book vaults of the library, and other vaults hold over 2 million valuable and historic manuscripts.

The small town of Victorville, about 50 miles inland, offers afficionados of the Western movie culture the opportunity to visit the Roy Rogers-Dale Evans Museum, in Seneca Road, and inspect the personal and professional memorabilia of the cowboy film star and childhood hero.

Below Los Angeles, between San Pedro and Redondo Beach, lies the Palos Verdes Peninsula, packed with enchanting beaches. It is also the location of Marineland, an impressive aquatic show complete with killer whales, sealions and dolphins, some living in a colony in their natural habitat.

Though adventurous visitors are allowed to swim in an aquarium shared by some 2,000 species of fish, volunteers must be at least four foot tall and weigh over five stone.

San Diego, near the Mexican border, the

A view across San Diego Bay, an important US Navy base, to North Island, and to the elegant curve of the Coronado Bay Bridge

with 151,000 people – is renowned for the monumental achievement of developing the navel orange. It also has an interesting Mission Inn on 7th Street which exhibits a collection of 900 bells among other Spanish antiques paintings, crosses and international dolls. In the chapel is a 200-year-old altar. Riverside accommodates a campus of California University on the eastern edge of the city.

About 20 miles south of Los Angeles is San Marino, where one of the world's

second largest city in California, is one of America's most modern and exciting towns. When the United States entered World War II, it became the new home of the Pacific Naval Headquarters, formerly based at Pearl Harbour. The effect was to attract not only shiploads of free-spending sailors and retired Navy men, but investment from new industry and commerce.

Radiating 20 miles north, south and east, San Diego's urban communities have spread from the coast to the desert. Its population of 789,000 is 125,000 more than San Francisco, although the one-and-a-half million people who inhabit its metropolitan area are only half the number living in the San Francisco conurbations.

As befits a city of that size San Diego has a busy airport, several self-contained communities, and Mission Bay – a 4,600-acre aquatic park. It also has a two-mile bridge over San Diego Bay linking the Coronado Peninsula with the downtown shopping areas. For tourists there are many attractions. The San Diego Zoo is one of the largest in the world, with over 3,200 animals of 800 species in captivity, and there are several good museums in Balboa Park, a 1,150-acre complex on the northeast edge of the business area. Not the least in interest is the Spreckels Organ Pavilion. It houses one of the largest outdoor organs in the world, which has 5,000 pipes.

Although San Diego is the most southerly city in California, the 13,500 people who live in Calexico and the Mexicans in Mexicali are like suburban neighbours. They are separated from each other by simply a

The Mission San Carlos Borromeo de Carmelo, established by Father Serra in 1771

fence. There are usually no problems about
arranging a trip across the border into
Mexico, but the United States control
points take more than a passing interest in
Mexican tourists, who may be illegal immigrants. The signs of Western affluence
vanish dramatically as soon as the Mexican
border is crossed from the United States.

The two countries at least share vast tracts
of desert. What American enterprise can do

with these arid wastes of land is demonstrated at Palm Springs in the Upper
Colorado desert. About equidistant from
San Diego and Los Angeles, overlooked by
the 10,786-foot San Jacinto Peak, Palm
Springs has been a popular spa for many
years. In this area, canyons are ten a penny.

The most interesting of them is Palm
Canyon, seven miles south on an Indian
Reservation, where over 3,000 palms –
some are believed to be more than 2,000
years old – line the canyon. It is possible to
drive there, but as the road is very narrow
the journey should be tackled with the
greatest caution.

An aerial tramway carries passengers two-
and-a-half miles, 6,000 feet up, from Valley
Station in Chino Canyon to Mountain
Station at the edge of Long Valley, where
spectacular views of the San Jacinto region
are spread out below. In Palm Springs
Desert Museum many interesting rock formations can be viewed, together with exhibits on art, natural science and the performing arts.

Despite Los Angeles' reputation for nur-
turing the most exotic human aspirations,
California in its widest sense is really one
gigantic nature reserve, where man's sophisticated ideas have little place. Once one
leaves the coast roads and starts to explore
the hinterland, mountains, valleys,
canyons, deserts and huge forests loom so
large that they have a breath-taking and
humbling effect on the visitor.

Further north-east beyond Desert Hot
Springs one enters typical California desert

*Palm Springs, the playground of the
wealthy and an oasis of luxury at the
foot of San Jacinto Peak in the upper
Colorado Desert*

country. Here mountain ranges rise to over
5,000 feet, striking granite formations flank
each side, and desert brush mingles with the
more spectacular and rare vegetation. Look
out for the Joshua Tree: its greenish-white
blossoms are at their most stunning in

March and April. In its honour a national monument has been marked out where tourists can camp in anyone of nine camp grounds. North-west and to the east of the Yucca Valley, a small settlement of 6,000 people inhabit an oasis between the Mojave and Colorado Deserts. The town of Twentynine Palms got its name when its boundary in the 1870s was marked out by a ring of 29 palms. Another unusual feature near the town is the United States Marine Corps Training Center – the largest in land area in the world. It lies four miles north of the town.

With its huge national parks California offers countless ways of getting lost in the wilds. Extremes in temperature, altitudes and terrain are common within short distances. In the Los Angeles area, it is possible at certain times of year to swim in the ocean and ski on fresh powder snow on the same day. The highest point on the American Continent (outside Alaska), the 14,495-foot-high Mount Whitney in Sequoia National Park about 80 miles west of Fresno, is also only about 85 miles from America's lowest point – in the mournfully named Death Valley National Monument. The spot is near Badwater, and lies 282 feet

Scotty's Castle at the northern edge of Death Valley was built by Walter P Scott, a performer in Buffalo Bill's Wild West Show

---

DEATH VALLEY

Hotels

FURNACE CREEK INN: On SR 190 one mile S of visitor centre, tel 786 2345. 67 rooms. Expensive.

FURNACE CREEK RANCH: On SR 190 adjacent to visitor centre, tel 786 2345. Moderate.

---

below sea level in the heart of the valley.

It earned its macabre name during the Gold Rush days when prospectors tried to use it as a short cut to the gold fields. Many perished in the attempt, but later roads were built strong enough to carry 20 mule teams and their cargo of boran. Some of the wagon loads weighed over 35 tons.

The valley fluctuates from a width of about four miles to about 16 miles and extends for 120 miles to rise to more than 11,000 feet at Telescope Peak. It is one of the hottest regions in the world, with daytime temperatures at times in excess of 120 degrees Fahrenheit. The highest temperature ever recorded was 190 degrees at Tule Spring on 12 July 1958, and the longest period during which temperatures hovered over the 100 degrees mark was for 126 days in the summer of 1959. Every year, however, temperatures during the summer are too intense for comfortable or safe travel through the valley without experienced guides and good equipment. It is usually

preferable to travel at night when temperatures are much lower. Predictably, it hardly ever rains there, and only two inches of rainfall are recorded on average every year. Even so, there are tempting springs which should be resisted for drinking purposes, unless the water has been sterilised.

The entire area of the Monument extends for nearly 3,000 square miles with 550 square miles of it below sea level. It is hard to believe that anyone would choose to live in such forbidding conditions. But Walter P Scott did, and the proof is in the Ruritanian folly he built among the gaunt boulders and parched soil of the valley.

A Wild West showman by profession, he was 30 when he vanished into Death Valley in 1902 to build himself a crude board shack for his home. Three years later he re-appeared in Los Angeles. Scotty and Los Angeles got on well together. A charismatic self-publicist, he hired the most expensive hotel suites, threw his money around ostentatiously and wherever he went, caused a stir that endeared him to the archetypal Angeleno. One day he vanished again – back to his beloved desert – but this time in the company of a Chicago multi-millionaire called Albert M Johnson. Together they lavished a fortune on constructing a castle 3,000 feet up in the most isolated region of the valley and close to the northern boundary of the Monument. They imported ornamental floor tiles from Spain and Italy, wrought-iron chandeliers from Germany and Austria and priceless paintings, tapestries and other furnishings from all over the world. In an upstairs music room they installed an organ which plays duets automatically with a grand piano, and hid the 1,600 pipes behind a cathedral grille. There are also 18 fireplaces, an 185-foot swimming pool and a fountain and fish pool in the living room. Johnson died in 1948, and when Scott died six years later, the foundation created by them to look after the place opened it to the public. Since then more than 150,000 visitors have made the pilgrimage to the estate.

As much of the state is dominated by its legacy of trees, the Sequoia and Kings Canyon National parks tell in their own way the story of nature's supremacy in California.

These gargantuan sequoia trees stud the landscape. The largest known stands 275 feet high in the Giant Forest. Aptly called General Sherman (a Civil War military commander who had a famous make of tank named after him), it has a circumference of 210 feet, and a mass of trunk filling 52,500 cubic feet. In the Grant and Redwood Mountain Groves in Kings Canyon another giant sequoia stands 267 feet high. Altogether California's plant life provides its parks with over 2,000 varieties of trees, shrubs and flowers.

Proceed for 11 miles out of Los Angeles city on Interstate 10 to Santa Monica.

Santa Monica
A residential seaside city, Santa Monica encompasses the beaches of Ocean Park, Will Rogers State Beach and the exclusive Malibu. Palisades Park, reached along the seafront cliffs, offers breathtaking views of the ever-blue Pacific, as do the many well-placed picnic spots and the specially designed viewpoints. The history of aviation is celebrated with a fine collection of scale-model aircraft and mementoes of famous fliers at the Donald Douglas Museum and Library at 2800 Airport Avenue.

Continue southwards along the unclassified coastal road for 5 miles to Marina del Rey.

Marina del Rey
Marina del Rey is home to Los Angeles' biggest marina, with sailing craft of all sizes berthed in its harbour. Boats for fishing and sailing can be hired from 13723 Fiji Way. Fishing is excellent here, with halibut, bass and bonito a-plenty just off this part of LA's shoreline. The first-time sailor may

Long Beach and the Magic Kingdom
2 days – 90 miles (plus ferry)

Los Angeles- Santa Monica – Marina del Rey – Redondo Beach – Palos Verdes – San Pedro – Long Beach – Santa Catalina Island – Newport Beach – Costa Mesa – Anaheim – Los Angeles

feel safe in the knowledge that a coastguard air-rescue service operates from this area. Speciality shops, restaurants and nightclubs are to be found in Fisherman's Village, on the seafront at 13755 Fiji Way.

Nine miles south along the coast is Redondo Beach.

Redondo Beach
Situated south of Santa Monica Bay, Redondo Beach is the site of an international surf festival which takes place annually in August. A popular resort, it offers the usual seaside attractions such as penny arcades and souvenir shops and,

for the seafood lover, fish stalls and seafood restaurants. All can be found on Monstad Pier at Fisherman's Wharf.

Proceed southwards along the coast to Palos Verdes Peninsula.

Palos Verdes Peninsula
Marineland, owned by 20th-Century Fox, is a world-famous extravaganza of performing killer whales, comic dolphins and acrobatic sealions. Snorkel divers are invited to dive into a massive 540,000-gallon tank where a trained diver-cum-tour guide will point out rare under-sea sights. The dive is relayed on a tv screen for the benefit of the less adventurous visitor. Wounded sea creatures are housed in a special

Marine Animal Care Center and looked after on the premises.

A playground, stage shows and picnic facilities ensure that young visitors won't be bored.

Continue on the coastal road for 7 miles to San Pedro.

San Pedro
Along with Wilmington and Terminal Island, San Pedro constitutes the Port of Los Angeles. The man-made harbour is one of the biggest deep-water ports in the country and it is guarded by one of America's major coastal defences, Fort MacArthur. A main attraction in San Pedro is the Ports O'Call Village, a replica 19th-century port community complete with gaslit streets and 'olde worlde' shops and restaurants. The Village is situated at the south end of Harbour Freeway, on the main channel of Los Angeles harbour. Narrated-tour cruises are operated daily.

During December or January excursions are available to watch the migrating grey whales.

Only 4 miles from San Pedro on the same unclassified coastal road is Long Beach.

Long Beach
California's sixth largest city, Long Beach is so-named because of the five-and-a-half-mile stretch of sandy beach which is one of its main tourist attractions. Long Beach Convention and Entertainment Center offers a varied programme of evening events from its two theatres and sporting and trade shows are held in an arena also housed in the Center. Excellent eating and shopping facilities can be found in Seaport Village at the end of Marina Drive, and at the Market Place on East Pacific Coast Highway. One of Britain's most famous luxury liners, the *Queen Mary*, is docked at Pier J off Long Beach. First launched in 1934, the 81,000-ton ship is now a floating museum. The main attractions on board are the 400 elegant state rooms which are now run as a luxury hotel, several excellent boutiques and restaurants, and famous underwater explorer Jacques Cousteau's Living Sea Museum which includes a shark tank. The ship's interior has been restored to its former elegance with as many as 57 different woods being used in the furnishing of cabins and gangways.

Three other typically 'British' attractions stand alongside the *Queen Mary* on the dockside – two gleaming red double-decker London buses and a traditional black taxi cab. These form part of

The palm-fringed sands of Santa Monica, lapped by the warm waters of the blue Pacific, one of many beaches within easy reach of Los Angeles

The most popular attraction in the resort town of Long Beach is the 'Queen Mary'. Her decks now house a hotel, restaurants and museums

a replica English village – over which the recorded chimes of Big Ben ring out every hour.

Continue southwards on State Route 1 to Newport Beach where you can catch the ferry (journey time 2 hours) across the 22-mile channel to Santa Catalina Island.

Santa Catalina Island
The sandy coves and crystal-clear waters of Santa Catalina Island were once the haunts of smugglers and pirates, but now the shores of this popular resort are only

darkened by the tourists who have been flocking here since the end of the last century. It became a fashionable haven for the rich and famous when chewing gum king William Wrigley bought the island in 1915.

Tours by glass-bottomed boat are available to visit the Californian State Marine Preserve where an exotic underwater world of rare marine plants, fishes and other forms of sea life can be enjoyed. In the evening, not to be missed, is a memorable boat trip to watch the world's largest flying fish at play. Water lovers will also find facilities for swimming, sailing, scuba-diving and fishing, while for landlubbers the flower-covered hills abound in walking, cycling or horse riding trails. Catalina's capital, Avalon, takes its name from that mystical isle of Celtic mythology to which King Arthur is said to have been transported after his death.

From Santa Catalina catch the ferry back to Newport Beach.

Newport Beach

The city of Newport Beach includes Linda Isle, Bay Shores, Harbor Island, Newport Heights, Corona del Mar, Lido Isle, Balboa Isle and Balboa, and boasts a population of over 64,000. Newport Harbor is a popular meeting place for yacht enthusiasts who come to attend the regattas held here almost every week-end. Visitors flock to this popular holiday resort which offers a beautiful six-mile stretch of sand with vistas of the warm, blue Pacific beyond.

On Upper Newport Bay is the Newport Dunes Aquatic Park which offers the visitor sports courts, amusements, picnicking facilities and a 20-acre lagoon.

Hotels

DEL WEBB'S NEWPORTER INN: 1107 Jamboree Rd, tel 644 1700. 325 rooms. Expensive.

NEWPORT BEACH MARRIOTT HOTEL: 900 Newport Center Dr, tel 640 4000. 377 rooms. Expensive.

NEWPORT CHANNEL INN: 6030 W Pacific Coast Hwy, tel 642 3030. 30 rooms. Moderate.

Restaurants

THE OLD SPAGHETTI FACTORY: 2110 Newport Blvd, tel 675 8654. Popular restaurant serving spaghetti with a wide choice of sauces. Inexpensive.

THE VELVET TURTLE: 59 Fashion Island, tel 644 5313. Steak, seafood and continental cuisine. Moderate.

About 2 miles away on the Pacific Coast is Costa Mesa.

Costa Mesa

Golf enthusiasts will remember Costa Mesa for its excellent municipal golf course, but for car freaks Briggs Cunningham's Automotive Museum at 250 East Baker Street will be the big attraction. An ex-racing driver and car constructor, Cunningham has around 100 classic, sports, and racing cars on show, some from as

Avalon Bay, Catalina Island. This tranquil and charming island retreat was the home of a Stone Age Indian culture as late as the 1600s

early as 1898. Pride of place is given to one of the largest and most expensive cars ever made – a 1927 Bugatti 'Royale'.

Drive 8 miles on the Costa Mesa Freeway to join the Santa Ana Freeway at Tustin. Proceed for 7 miles to Anaheim.

Anaheim

Not so much a town, more of a kingdom, Anaheim plays host to 74 acres of 'Magic Kingdom' – the famous Disneyland. Disneyland comprises seven theme parks, each one with different adventures and attractions, plus shops, restaurants, snack bars and souvenir stalls. The entrance at 1313 Harbour Boulevard leads into 'Main Street' – a reconstruction of a typical 1890s smalltown thoroughfare which is paraded by favourite Disney characters like Donald Duck and Pluto. At Main Street Depot old-fashioned locomotives are waiting to take visitors on a tour of the park. Unless you have an unlimited timetable, it is wise, at this point, to choose which 'lands' are of greatest interest and head for them, as a complete tour is likely to last several days. Themes range from the good old days of 'Main Street' to the futuristic 'Tomorrowland', a space-age extravaganza with a feast of electronic and aeronautical exhibits. You can ride a rocket to the moon from spectacular Space Mountain and then, while still seeing stars, head for 'Fantasyland', dominated by

Sleeping Beauty's Castle. Back in America's colourful history is 'Frontierland'; enclosed by a log stockade, it takes visitors back to the days of pioneer exploration. You can ride a mule train through forests and deserts where electronically-animated birds, animals and reptiles roam, or explore a gold mine and take the stern-wheeler 'Mark Twain' around Tom Sawyer Island. One of the most popular attractions in Disneyland is the jungle cruise in 'Adventureland' – a terrifying trail past hippos, elephants, alligators and spear-throwing cannibals. A

swashbuckling performance by the Pirates of the Caribbean ends with a spectacular dynamite explosion.

In 'New Orleans' Square', the Southern city's great heyday of the mid-19th century is effectively re-created, and there is a spooky Haunted Mansion here, complete with 999 ghosts. The kingdom's latest addition is 'Bear Country'; reached by canoe, it is a country-style jamboree inspired by the exploits of early explorers like Davy Crockett.

Continue on the Santa Ana Freeway (Interstate 5) for 22 miles to Los Angeles city.

Fabulous Disneyland, a kaleidoscope of fantasy and fun dedicated to the business of giving pleasure to young and old alike

Hollywood to San Simeon

3 days – 440 miles

Los Angeles – Hollywood – San Fernando – Newhall – Valencia –
Lebec – San Miguel – San Simeon – San Luis Obispo – Lompoc –
Solvang – Santa Barbara – Ventura – Port Hueneme – Malibu –
Pacific Palisades – Beverly Hills – Los Angeles

From Los Angeles proceed on
the US101 to Hollywood.

Hollywood
The Hollywood dream factory
belongs to everyone. Although
today many of the famous film
studios have left, and the 1930s
architecture is somewhat run-
down, there is still a magic about
these streets that yesterday were
paved with gold. The undisputed
glamour capital of the world,
Hollywood gave entertainment to
millions via the silver screen.

Visitors can relive Hollywood in its
heyday by joining the tours
through 'back lots' and sound
stages of motion picture studios,
that take place regularly at
Burbank and Universal City.
Highlights of these tours include
special-effects demonstrations,
stunt shows and set construction.
On Hollywood Boulevard there are
1,500 bronze stars, each one
commemorating a different screen
idol, set into the pavement. At
6925 Hollywood Boulevard is
perhaps the most famous, and

HOLLYWOOD TO SAN SIMEON

certainly the most visited site, Mann's Chinese Theatre. The scene of glittering premieres attended by glamorous stars, dripping in diamonds and charm, Mann's is a museum in its own right. For here, in 1927, a star called Norma Talmadge started a trend that many more familiar show business celebrities were to follow. She set her hands and footprints in concrete, and today visitors can match their hands and feet with those of Errol Flynn, Rita Hayworth and many more.

At 2301 North Highland Avenue is the Hollywood Bowl, a natural amphitheatre in the foothills, with a gigantic stadium designed by one of the country's most famous architects, Frank Lloyd Wright.

From Hollywood take the Hollywood Freeway and the Interstate 5 (the Golden State Freeway) for 15 miles, then proceed on State Route 118 for 5 miles east into San Fernando.

San Fernando

A fine example of one of the 21 missions founded by Father Junipero Serra, Mission San Fernando Rey de Espana was founded in 1797 and boasts a restored church and monastery. Brand Park, the old gardens, abounds with shrubs and flowers that grew originally in the gardens of the other 20 missions.

Take Interstate 210 from San Fernando and drive for 5 miles to Interstate 5; north on Interstate 5 for 2 miles to State Route 14. Continue on State Route 14 for 2 miles, from there take the unclassified road into Newhall.

Newhall

Now a county park, Newhall was once the home of late Western star William S Hart. Amid the original furnishings of the Hart residence are displays of Indian and western artefacts and other items of historical interest. The ranch covers some 253 acres where visitors may picnic or just enjoy the view and watch the bison graze. The house is open to the public at weekends and on certain days of the week; the park is open daily.

From Newhall take the unclassified road to Interstate 5 and proceed for 5 miles north into Valencia.

Valencia

Children can have a fun time in Valencia at the Six Flags Magic Mountain on Magic Mountain Parkway. Covering 200 acres, this mammoth playground and entertainment complex offers such attractions as two roller coasters called 'Revolution' and 'Colossus', a theatre, craft demonstrations and live music shows.

Continue north on Interstate 5 into Lebec.

Lebec

An interesting museum in Lebec takes the form of a restored US Army Dragoon post. It was used in 1854–64 by the US Camel Corps who transported supplies all the way from San Antonio, Texas, between 1857 and 1861.

From Lebec travel north on Interstate 5 and State Route 99 for 40 miles to Bakersfield and continue for 20 miles north to the Famoso interchange and proceed westwards on State Route 46 for approximately 88 miles to US 101. Take US 101 north into San Miguel.

San Miguel

Magnificent frescoes, dating from 1821, can be seen in the Mission San Miguel Archangel which is now in use as a parish church. The third Sunday in September is the time of San Miguel's annual fiesta.

Retrace your path south on US 101 for 9 miles to Paso Robles, then take State Route 46 west for 26 miles to join State Route 1. Continue north on State Route 1 for approximately 12 miles into San Simeon.

The Hollywood Bowl, the summer home of the Los Angeles Philharmonic, is a vast amphitheatre lying at the foot of the Hollywood Hills

San Simeon

Perched atop La Cuesta Encantada (the enchanted hill) in the Santa Lucia Mountains, San Simeon is renowned for its connections with the late newspaper tycoon William Randolph Hearst. The subject of Orson Wells' most famous early work, *Citizen Kane*, Hearst owned a fabulous estate which incorporates a twin-towered Hispano-Moorish castle, La Casa Grande, where Hearst lived, along with his 50 million dollar art collection. The castle, with its sumptuously-decorated 100 rooms, guesthouses (also furnished in grand style), and the landscaped Italian gardens complete with pools, statues and fountains, are part of the San Simeon State Historical Monument.

Hotels

BEST WESTERN GREEN TREE INN: $3\frac{1}{2}$ miles S on SR 1, tel 927 4691. 62 rooms. Moderate.

EL REY INN: 206 E Frontage Rd, tel 927 3998. 40 rooms. Moderate.

SAN SIMEON LODGE: $3\frac{1}{2}$ miles S on SR 1, tel 927 4601. 63 rooms. Moderate.

Restaurant

THE HAMLET: 206A E Frontage Rd, tel 927 3087. Well-prepared food is served in this small, charming restaurant. Moderate.

Follow coastal State Route 1 for about 40 miles to San Luis Obispo.

The delightful beaches below San Simeon are usually less crowded than those further south

San Luis Obispo

The quaint old town of San Luis Obispo, nestling in the Los Padres mountains, was built around the 18th-century white-walled adobe, Mission San Luis Obispo de Tolosa. Known as the 'Prince of Missions', it was the first to use tiled roofing as a deterrent against the Indians who used to set fire to the original rush roofs. Now the local parish church and museum, relics of its mission days and exhibits relating to the Cherokee and Chumash Indian culture can be seen here. A secluded creek runs by the foot of the mission gardens.

Reminders of the pioneer days still exist here in the form of the Sinsheimer Drygoods Store, founded in 1876 and still selling the same kind of goods today. The premises have the original cast-iron colonnaded façade which was made in San Francisco over 100 years ago. Another pioneering family came from Canton in search of gold and opened the Al Louis Store in 1874. It still stands today, and specializes in Oriental merchandise.

Also of interest is the County Historical Museum, with its wonderful collection of folklore. Of particular fascination is a book, dated 1853, called *The Matchmaker*, which gave the locals valuable advice, on among other things, how to 'woo, win and wed' or, failing that, how to have pleasant dreams.

Follow south US 101 to Grover City, then take State Route 1 to Orcutt where the road becomes County Route S20. Continue on this road into Lompoc

Lompoc

Summer is a colourful time in Lompoc, when the flower-seed fields, for which the town is famous, are in full bloom. Summertime also sees regular demonstrations of traditional crafts here. La Purisma Mission was rebuilt by Franciscan priests after it had been reduced to ruins by an earthquake.

From Lompoc follow State Route 246 for 15 miles to Solvang.

Solvang

In 1911 Solvang, known nowadays as 'Little Denmark', was established as a settlement for Danish immigrants. The Scandinavian style is prevalent in the town's architecture, and Danish festivals are held here during September. California's first seminars took place here at the beautifully-restored Santa Ines Mission (founded 1804). Picnic facilities are available beside the impressive rushing waters of the Nojoqui Falls, a few miles south-west of Solvang.

Continue southward along the coast on US 101 past Goleta, an attractive coastal town surrounded by lemon groves, to Santa Barbara 20 miles away.

Santa Barbara

Standing on a narrow shelf between the magnificent Santa Ynes Mountains and the Pacific Coast, is the picturesque Spanish-style town of Santa Barbara.

Now a thriving holiday resort, Santa Barbara retains a Spanish influence that has existed here since 1782. The original classical adobe-style buildings were destroyed by an earthquake in 1925 but the whole town was rebuilt in the traditional fashion using warmly-coloured stucco and terra-cotta tiles made from unfired, sun-dried materials. Each dwelling is crowned with rounded red clay roof tiles, carefully moulded by Indian women, on their thighs. Many of these houses are still inhabited today. Another reminder of Santa Barbara's Spanish heritage can be found in the vine-hung streets with names such as Los Olivos (The Olives) and Camino Cielo (Street of the Sky).

The County Courthouse at 1120 Aracapa Street boasts a fine

The Santa Barbara Mission stands aloof on a hilltop above the town. Its beauty has earned it the name 'Queen of the Missions'

The J Paul Getty Museum at Malibu, in which is housed priceless Greek and Roman sculptures and Renaissance and Baroque paintings

example of Spanish–Moorish decoration as well as interesting murals and a sunken garden.

Towering high above the city and sea is the Mission Santa Barbara in whose halls excellent examples of Greek, Roman and Egyptian sculptures can be found. In August a 'Little Fiesta' is held here. Behind the Mission, in a little wooded canyon, lies the Museum of Natural History, at 2559 Puesta de Sol Road, where mounted specimens of the California Condor, America's largest flying bird, are on show.

Hotels

AMBASSADOR BY THE SEA MOTEL: 202 W Cabrillo Blvd, tel 965 4577. 30 rooms. Moderate.

EL PATIO-BEST WESTERN MOTOR HOTEL: 336 W Cabrillo Blvd and Castillo St, 965 6556. 60 rooms. Moderate.

MIRAMAR MOTOR HOTEL RESORT: 3 miles E adjacent to US 101, San Ysidro Rd exit, tel 969 2203. 200 rooms. Moderate-expensive.

Restaurants

THE FEED STORE: 110 Santa Barbara St, tel 966 2435. Interior designed as an old feed and grain store. Informal and casual atmosphere. Moderate-expensive.

OLIVE MILL BISTRO – IN MONTECITO: 1295 Coast Village Rd, tel 969 4900. European cuisine. Expensive.

Drive alongside the palm-fringed beaches of Santa Barbara and continue for 60 miles along the beautifully-landscaped freeway US 101 into Ventura.

Ventura

One of California's oldest towns, Ventura was once the site of a Chumash Indian settlement. Nowadays it boasts all the attractions of a seaside holiday town, including a public pier and marina and beautiful beaches.

The influence on the town of Indian, Spanish and early settlers can be appreciated by a visit to the Ventura County Historical Museum (closed Mondays) at 100 East Main Street. An agricultural display in the grounds is also of interest. Pioneering Franciscan

Padre, Father Junipero Serra, walked nearly 5,000 miles and founded 21 missions along the Californian coast before he died in 1784. Ventura's Mission San Buenaventura was his final offering.

On Mission Hill stands the Padre Serra Cross, where the first one was erected by Father Serra. Easter services take place here at sunrise, and impressive views can be enjoyed from this point.

Continue on US 101 and State Route 1 for 20 miles then descend southwards toward the coast and Port Hueneme.

One of many strange and exotic houses found in Beverly Hills, the traditional home of Hollywood's 'stars of the silver screen'

Port Hueneme

Part of the US Naval Construction Battalion, the Civil Engineer Corps/Seabee Museum exhibits models of CEC and Seabee equipment and uniforms, as well as weapons and paintings of battle scenes. A free visitor's pass is obtainable at the Ventura Gate.

Proceed south on State Route 1 and continue for approximately 30 miles to Malibu.

Malibu

In the shadow of the Santa Monica Mountains lie mile upon mile of magnificent golden sandy beaches washed by giant breakers known to surf riders all over the world; this is Malibu.

Writers and artists are drawn to the beauty of these shores and the sun-bronzed bodies of surfing beach boys are a familiar sight. Film stars and members of the 'jet-set' have homes here, where in the 1920s Hollywood's movie set held their legendary wild parties. The J Paul Getty Museum at 17985 Pacific Coast Highway exhibits the collection of art treasures amassed over a long lifetime by the late oil magnate. Housed in a marble re-creation of the Villa dei Papyri which was buried in lava when Vesuvius erupted in AD 79, the museum has been nicknamed 'Pompeii-by-the-Pacific'. Greek and Roman sculptures figure strongly but there is also a fine collection of French, Italian and Dutch paintings.

Continue along State Route 1 for 10 miles into Pacific Palisades.

Pacific Palisades

Now a State Historic Park, 14253 Sunset Boulevard was formerly the home of the late humorist and film star Will Rogers. The house and grounds, covering 186 acres, are now open daily to the public.

Take the local road to Sunset Boulevard then proceed for 12 miles into Beverly Hills.

Beverly Hills

The acres of sumptuous homes of many film and television stars has made Beverly Hills the most famous residential suburb in southern California. Visitors wishing to identify the homes of the stars may take one of the various bus and limousine tours or, alternatively, they may go it alone with the help of a free walking tour pamphlet, issued by the Southern California Visitors' Council at 705 West 7th Street.

Drive east for 10 miles on Sunset Boulevard to State Route 2, which connects with Hollywood Freeway for the return to the centre of Los Angeles.

Los Angeles

Unlike any other American city, and yet one of the most American in character, Los Angeles is a strange, sprawling megalopolis of many suburbs, united early in this century by the need to take advantage of a water supply from Owens River. The result is a number of distinct communities united beneath a common umbrella to create California's biggest city.

A few Mexican farmers founded the city in the latter half of the 18th century, but by the 1800s the Franciscan friars who at first dominated the area were complaining that the citizens were paying 'more attention to gambling and playing the guitar than to tilling their lands and educating their children.'

Los Angeles has never quite managed to shrug off such an image. The rise of Hollywood enforced it, although in reality the citrus-fruit-growing industry was just as important in the city's early development.

But Los Angeles is a place where dreams come true, where the entrepreneur comes to explore new ground, the creative come to experiment, the labourer comes in search of a better way of life.

This city of broad boulevards, palm-planted parks and gleaming new buildings was created by opportunists, and remains a city of opportunity.

▼ *The City of Los Angeles sprawls across 464 square miles of California's countryside, but green and pleasant parks such as this give colour and cool shade to this seemingly endless urban jungle*

LOS ANGELES

There is no way that Los Angeles can live up to the reputation Hollywood, its famous, sprawling, brash suburb, has spent more than 70 years acquiring for it. Hollywood (see page 41), motivated by steely, commercial resolve to make one box-office success after another, has not only effectively over-shadowed the rest of the 80-odd communities which make up Los Angeles, but in the process invested the city with a fairytale glamour it doesn't need or deserve.

The city is a conglomeration of settlements which grew up over 200 years around a stretch of magnificent sandy beaches. Now spreading across 464 square miles, Los Angeles is America's third largest city, with a metropolitan population of more than seven million. In the heart of the city, there are more than two-and-a-half-million people, helping to make it in size and area the biggest in California.

The rest of the population live in gigantic self-contained conurbations like Long Beach, Glendale, Pasadena and Santa Monica. Burbank, which is almost synonymous with Hollywood, having become the home of several important film and TV studios, sustains a population of 85,000 – thanks in part to the growth of the aviation industry in the area.

There is really no end to Los Angeles. Some people might also say that there was never much of a beginning to it either.

Jack Smith, the distinguished columnist of the *Los Angeles Times*, once said of the city he has loved and lovingly criticised for more than 20 years: 'I have to keep reminding myself that the city had a pastoral beginning, and was not created overnight by some dreadful Southern Pacific train wreck!'

Pastoral its beginning certainly was. Eleven Spanish families, making up a total population of 44, set up El Pueblo De Nuestra Senora La Reina de Los Angeles de Porciuncula (which means 'the village of our lady the Queen of the Angels of Porciuncula'), on the site where Los Angeles now stands, in 1781.

In its predictable preoccupation with the past, a trait it shares with most of America's leading cities, Los Angeles lays claim to antiquity. At the Rancho La Brea Tar Pits, on Wilshire Boulevard and Curson Avenue, one of the world's richest sources of Ice-Age fossils is carefully preserved in the George C Page La Brea Discoveries Museum.

Sabretooth tigers, wolves, birds and horses – reconstruction of Ice-Age animals – are on show, and in the La Brea Story Theaters, 15-minute documentary

◄ *Downtown's most distinctive landmark, the Bonaventure Hotel, whose vast lobby shelters a one-acre lake*

▼ *A winner with the children – the narrow-gauge railway at Knott's Berry Farm*

films and slide-shows dramatise prehistoric life in the area. Outside, where the sticky asphalt beds entrapped prehistoric plant and animal life, a strategically placed viewing platform gives an idea of how the specimens were discovered.

The El Pueblo de Los Angeles State Historic Park contains within its 44 acres bounded by Main, Arcadia, Los Angeles and Macy streets, remnants of a great deal of the city's more recent past. Olvera Street, the oldest street in the city, is part of the park, and on it stands the oldest house, Avila Adobe, built around 1818 and open to the public. The Pico House, erected in 1869, can also be viewed, but on a guided tour only. It contains traces of the elegant hotel it once was, and of its resourceful original owner, the last Mexican Governor of California.

Los Angeles' most significant history, however, belongs to the 20th century. It was in the first years of the 1900s that the advantages of the mild West Coast weather drew the young pioneering film makers to Hollywood. Many had earlier set up a temporary centre for their bizarre activities in Chicago and New York, but the first film maker on the West Coast was Colonel William Selig, who shot the screen version of *The Count of Monte Cristo* around Los Angeles in 1907. He was followed soon after by several other ambitious would-be movie moguls, and the first operational film studio in Los Angeles opened in 1911 at Blondeau's Tavern. This has since become rather better known as Paramount Pictures. With Columbia and Universal Studios, Paramount still turns out major films for the cinema. Most of the other big names have either gone, or are concentrating on television and advertising films.

At Universal Studios, on the Hollywood freeway at Lankershim Boulevard, they have gone one better. They have turned the 420-acre studio lot into a giant Barnum and Bailey-style fairground, with some of the more memorable creations of recent film and

television spectaculars on show. If you want close acquaintance with the shark in *Jaws* the tour will give you an eye-to-eye confrontation with the plastic, toothy monster and the mechanism that made him work. On the other hand, you can happily endure a mock enactment of a typical scene from the science-fiction film, *Battlestar Galactica*, or shake the very lifeless hand of the *Incredible Hulk*. In a four-and-a-half-hour tour of the lot on the Glamortram you will even survive a bridge collapsing under the weight of the tram as you pass over it. You can also take part in a new scene for the 1970s disaster movie, *Airport*, which is video-taped and inserted into the original film before it is shown to the audience. More than $3\frac{1}{2}$ million people have taken Universal Studios into their itinerary since the astute movie makers of Universal decided that there was perhaps as much to be made from asking people to pay for the privilege of watching them make films as there was from the actual film-making itself. A Stunt Show, an Animal Actors Theater and a Make-Up Show are other attractions especially geared to young visitors, and there are numerous side shows.

Rather different in its approach to drawing the crowds is Disneyland (see page 40). Though about 25 miles out of the centre of Los Angeles at Anaheim, it belongs to Hollywood and Los Angeles as assuredly as Mickey Mouse and Donald Duck. It was here that Walt Disney developed a new kind of fantasy world, based on the captivating characters who had populated his films since the 1930s. More than 200 million people have made the pilgrimage to Disneyland since it opened in 1955. On the first day there were 30,000, and the first year more than a hundred times that number went through the turnstiles. By 1980 the annual figure had risen to $11\frac{1}{2}$ million. The number of attractions in the park has also increased. Now there are seven theme parks, among them Bear Country, Frontierland, Adventureland and Tomor-

▲ *Watts Towers, built from scrap by Simon Rodia, a tilesetter. At first ridiculed, the towers are now regarded as works of art*

◄ *Sleeping Beauty's Castle, in Fantasyland, perhaps the most famous of Disneyland attractions*

▼ *The Mexican Market in Olvera Street, one of the oldest thoroughfares in Los Angeles*

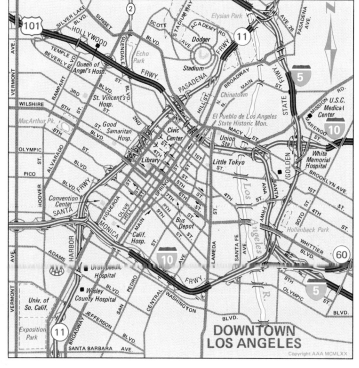

rowland. They are linked by a whispering, gleaming two-and-a-half-mile monorail system – the first of its kind in the world – operating at roof-top height.

Disneyland is as much a playground for adults as it is for children, as the queues at most of the major attractions testify. For ingenuity and spectacle, Space Mountain, a roller coaster ride through the cosmos, is an unrivalled gravity-defying ordeal apparently appealing equally to all ages (but mercifully barred to children below a certain height and weight for safety reasons).

A few miles away, Knott's Berry Farm is a rival entertainment complex, but here the theme is more rustic, and its novelties have a distinctly Wild West flavour. The farm, though principally a commercial amusement park, still turns out branded products, particularly from its orchards, and sells all manner of preserves all over the world. Its best-known speciality is Boysen Berry Jam made from the fruit of a plant which is a cross between a blackberry, loganberry and raspberry. Rudolph Boysen discovered the hybrid and his friends Walter and Cordelia Knott first grew the plant on their 20 acres of land in the 1920s. Knott's Berry Farm has its share of sophisticated thrills – don't miss a monstrous roller coaster called Montezuma's Revenge which loops the loop at breakneck speed, or the controlled jump from a parachute tower.

There are several other entertainment complexes in the Los Angeles area (see Directory), and like much else in southern California, they are within easy driving reach – thanks to the city's extensive multi-lane freeway network.

Sweeping in giant curves over the city these massive, snake-like ribbons of concrete are the very arteries of Los Angeles. Long before urban highways became a necessity in other major cities, Los Angeles started to build its 620 miles of city freeways. The concept of personal transport is developed to the full in Los Angeles. At the last count there was one car for every 1.8 residents – yet the monumental traffic congestion such a statistic would presage miraculously never quite seems to happen along the freeways or in the streets below. Even in downtown, the commercial heart of Los Angeles, the evening rush-hour passes smoothly enough, the clamour of the homeward bound traffic soon giving way to the echoing silence of the ominously deserted streets.

Downtown, where the streets have charming names like Geranium, Flower, Hope, Grand and Spring, is now a concentration of high-rise buildings with shining façades and imposing credentials. Along Figueroa Street is the Atlantic Richfield Plaza, a rabbit warren of underground shopping malls which is one of the world's largest underground shopping centres. Above ground, a 52-floor twin-towered office complex dominates much of its surroundings. In contrast, most of the buildings in Los Angeles are low-rise and not very impressive. They are the result of the years when skyscrapers were banned in this notorious earthquake-prone city.

Until the 1960s, the limit was 13 floors – a regulation strictly observed except by the builders of the City Hall which, like the Beanstalk, grew and grew into a giant of 28 storeys. Although public places occasionally display notices advising visitors not to use lifts in cases of fire or earthquakes, nobody

seriously likes to think about the prospect of tremors, or the disaster the San Andreas fault along the California coast could wreak in a bad shake as it did in San Francisco in 1906. The subject as a topic of conversation is almost as taboo as talk about the profligate Hollywood era of star worship.

The only profitable activity to survive from that glamorous world are the coach tours which pause outside the sumptuous homes where the giants of the silver screen once lived. Even Sunset Boulevard is not what it was, but for the faithful followers of the stardom trail, there are still plenty of reminders of the magic years when Beverly Hills, Santa Monica, Malibu and Pacific Palisades were part of a fairy-tale world. Surprisingly there are no Clark Gable boulevards, no Gary Cooper avenues, no Mary Pickford parks, or Marilyn Monroe monuments in Los Angeles (though there is a John Wayne Airport in Orange Country, where he had lived most of his life, and a recently erected statue of John Lennon, the murdered ex-Beatle, outside City Hall). There are not even theatres or public buildings in Hollywood or Beverly Hills built in the memory of these unofficial ambassadors of the American way of life.

Los Angeles however is not without its artistic amenities. The Hollywood Bowl was for many years the principal cultural mecca of the city. Seating more than 17,000 people outdoors in an amphitheatre, it opened in March 1921 to the chorus of Wagner's *Parsifal*. This summer home of the Los Angeles Symphony Orchestra stands at the foot of the Hollywood Hills in a park of 116 acres, attractively laid out with 2,000 trees and numerous fountains. At night it is floodlit. Since the 1960s, the Los Angeles Music Center in the Civic Center Mall has provided a base for the orchestra's winter season. Concerts, operas, recitals and dance programmes are staged at the 3,000-seater Dorothy Chandler Pavilion all year round. The Pavilion, its sculptured fluted columns faced in white quartz and lit by Bavarian crystal chandeliers, is one of three in the Center, and has helped Los Angeles to rebut the imputation that it is a 'a cultural wasteland'. Others have showered it with epithets like 'Cuckooland' and 'Moronia'. None of them is fair comment, although the showbiz razzmatazz of so much of the Los Angeles lifestyle has not helped its reputation.

▲ *The curios shops and restaurants in Chinatown are particularly appealing at night*

▶ *Gunfights are acted out for the benefit of visitors on the film sets of Universal Studios*

▲ *A replica of a mastodon, whose fossilised remains were found in the Rancho La Brea Tar Pits in Hancock Park*

▼ *Mann's Chinese Theater, renowned for the hand and foot prints set into the forecourt*

Nowhere but in Los Angeles could the burial industry flourish with such entrepreneurial gusto. At one of the four famous Forest Lawn Memorial Parks, they sell funeral arrangements like estate houses, assuring prospective buyers in deadpan prose that 'because everything is under one management, costs are lower'. The main Forest Lawn in South Glendale Avenue consists of 300 acres on which stand three churches and a museum filled with stained-glass, marble statues and a biblical coin collection. There are also audio-visual presentations of bible scenes. Charmingly simplistic in their approach, all the Forest Lawns are worth visiting, if only for the treasures displayed there. Other parks and gardens in the city have more obvious tourist appeal. At Griffith Park, the largest municipal park in America, an observatory, a 500-seat planetarium, a laserium, and a hall of science stand on 4,000 acres on the slopes of Mount Hollywood. It also has a zoo, with over 2,000 mammals, bird and reptiles distributed over 113 acres. Here you can visit a bird sanctuary, patronise the Greek Theater where popular shows are staged, ride on a historic old locomotive in a transport museum called Travel Town, play golf or tennis, run on an athletic track or walk on trails studded with picnic sites.

Further afield, at the end of a 50-minute run on the appropriate freeway, the city of Long Beach (see page 38), part of the Los Angeles area, offers two colossal distractions in its harbour – the 81,000-ton Cunard liner *Queen Mary*, and beside it, eccentric millionaire Howard Hughes' giant flying boat, *The Spruce Goose*. Both are relics of an era when big was synonymous with beautiful. Sixteen dockside acres had to be cleared to provide easy access and adequate parking for the 10 million visitors who have already boarded the *Queen Mary* since it was permanently anchored in the custom-built 900-foot dock in 1967.

In her new career, the *Queen Mary*, holder of the Blue Riband Atlantic speed record, has become a floating museum. Two of her decks had to be ripped out to accommodate the hundreds of exhibits in several maritime collections, and in 1980 her hull was repainted for the first time in 13 years. Much of the *Queen Mary*'s luxurious 1930s décor and furnishings have been carefully restored. Though the first-class deck and cabins have become a 400-roomed luxury hotel, the graciousness of the period has been carefully preserved.

Unlike the *Queen Mary*, which sailed the Atlantic for 30 years, *The Spruce Goose* only flew once, and was then not seen in public again for 30 years.

It seems appropriate that what was once the largest liner in the world, and the greatest flying ship ever built should, long after their heyday, be drawing the crowds again. Thanks to Hollywood, Los Angeles is accustomed to putting on a good show. Whatever else it has been called, it enjoys the name of 'The Entertainment Capital of the World'.

Los Angeles Directory

either expensive, moderate or inexpensive. All have bathrooms and colour television.

HOTELS

The hotels listed here are either recommended by the American Automobile Association (AAA) or have been selected because of their particular appeal to tourists. As a rough guide to cost, they have been classified as

BEL AIR SANDS HOTEL: 11461 Sunset Blvd, tel 476 6571. 162 rooms. Facilities include putting, wading pool and two tennis courts. Entertainment. Expensive.

BEVERLY HILLS HOTEL: 9641 Sunset Blvd, Beverly Hills, tel 276 2251. 325 rooms. The Polo Lounge is LA's most exclusive watering-hole, and the Coterie Restaurant is one of the best. Expensive.

BEVERLY HILLCREST: Pico Blvd, Beverly Hills, tel 277 2800. 150 rooms. A well-furnished hotel, with splendid views over the city to the ocean. Swimming pool. Two restaurants. Moderate.

BEVERLY HILTON HOTEL: 9876 Wilshire Blvd, tel 274 7777. 634 rooms. Services include heated pool, colour TVs and movies. Both the Polo Lounge Bar and the Coterie Restaurant are noted night-spots. Expensive.

BILTMORE HOTEL: 515 S Olive St at 5th St, tel 624 1911.

1,000 rooms. On Downtown LA's doorstep, the Biltmore has a reputation for style and service. Bernard's Restaurant is equally revered. Expensive.

BONAVENTURE: 350 S Figueroa St, tel 624 1000. 1,500 rooms. An outstanding hotel with five golden towers gracing the Los Angeles skyline. Included in the complex are rooftop bars, shopping arcades and a lake. Expensive.

CENTURY PLAZA HOTEL: 2025 Av of the Stars, tel 277 2000. 750 rooms. All the services and entertainment that you

would expect from a top hotel. Expensive.

DEL CAPRI HOTEL: 10587 Wilshire Blvd, tel 474 3511. 80 rooms. Set in attractive grounds with its own heated pool. Moderate.

FIGUEROA HOTEL: 939 S Figueroa St, tel 627 8971. Centrally-placed hotel offering quality and comfort at a reasonable price. Inexpensive.

GLENDALE MOTEL: 1531 Colorado St, tel 243 7126. 10 rooms. Comfortable hotel in the NE of the city. No pets. Inexpensive.

HACIENDA HOTEL: 525 Sepulveda Blvd, tel 322 1212. 660 rooms. Various facilities including heated pools, movies and laundry, plus airport transport service. Moderate.

HOWARD JOHNSON'S MOTOR LODGE: 5990 Green Valley Circle, tel 641 7740. 200 rooms. Heated pool and coin laundry. Airport shuttle service. Moderate.

HYATT REGENCY: 711 S Hope St, tel 683 1234. 487 rooms. Two dining rooms, movies, entertainment and rooftop bar. Expensive.

HYATT WILSHIRE: 3315 Wilshire Blvd, tel 381 7411. 400 rooms. Facilities include pay movies, valet garage and evenings-only restaurant, plus entertainment. Expensive.

LOS ANGELES HILTON: 930 Wilshire Blvd, tel 629 4321. 1,200 rooms. Excellent accommodation with heated pool, movies and a valet garage. Entertainment. Expensive.

MAYFLOWER HOTEL: 535 S Grand Av, tel 624 1331. 350 rooms. Good, old-fashioned comfort. Moderate.

NEW OTANI HOTEL: 120 S Los Angeles St, tel 629 1200. 448 rooms. Charming Japanese hotel in lovely gardens styled on its namesake in Tokyo. Sauna and massage. Entertainment. Expensive.

OASIS MOTEL: 2200 W Olympic Blvd, tel 385 4191. 70 rooms. Pleasant-roomed hotel situated in a quiet part of town. Heated pool. Inexpensive.

OLYMPIAN HOTEL: 1903 W Olympic Blvd, tel 385 7141. 150 rooms. Comfortable hotel with pool, restaurant and coffee-shop. Inexpensive.

RAINBOW HOTEL: 536 S Hope St, tel 627 9941. Quiet hotel located in the business area of the city. Inexpensive.

SHERATON PLAZA LA REINA: 6101 W Century Blvd, tel 642 1111. 827 rooms. Modern hotel opened in 1981. Heated pool and airport transport service. Moderate.

UNIVERSITY HILTON: 3540 S Figueroa St, tel 748 1531. 241 rooms. Heated pool, suites and pay parking. Regular entertainment. Expensive.

WINONA MOTEL: 5131 Hollywood Blvd, tel 663 1243. 23 rooms. Comfortable hotel with heated pool. Inexpensive.

RESTAURANTS

The restaurants listed below have been chosen either because they are recommended by the American Automobile Association (AAA) or for their appeal to tourists. They have been classified as either expensive, moderate, or inexpensive as a rough guide to cost.

BERNARD'S (BILTMORE HOTEL): 515 S Olive St, tel 624 0183. Excellent French restaurant specialising in seafood. Superb service and eye-catching décor. Expensive.

BROWN DERBY RESTAURANTS: 1628 Vine St, Hollywood, tel 469 5151; 9537 Wilshire Blvd, tel 276 2311. The original Brown Derby on Wilshire Blvd is partly-shaped as a Derby hat. The popular American speciality Cobb salad started life here. Moderate.

CHIANTI: 7383 Melrose Av, tel 653 8333. Small Italian restaurant with a romantic atmosphere. Fine cuisine. Moderate.

EL CHOLO MEXICAN RESTAURANT: 112 S Western Av, tel 734 2773. A dining-house opened back in the 1920s. Menu features crabmeat enchilada and other Mexican specialities. Inexpensive.

EMILIO'S: 6602 Melrose Av, tel 935 4922. Elegant Italian restaurant located in the city centre. Fine pasta and seafood. Expensive.

FAMOUS ENTERPRISE FISH CO: 174 Kinney St, Santa Monica, tel 392 8366. Mainly Mexican-style shellfish and other seafood, charcoal-grilled. Moderate.

FRANCOIS: on C-level of Atlantic Richfield Plaza, Flower St, tel 680 2727. Predominantly French cuisine served in plush surroundings. Cocktails. Pay garage. Expensive.

GULLIVER'S: 13181 Mindanao Way, tel 821 8866. Reasonably priced meals served in an English-style restaurant. Varied luncheon menu but prime ribs only for dinner.

Reservation advised. Moderate.

HARRY'S RESTAURANT & DELI: 416 West 7th St, tel 622 3311. A wide range of delicatessen food in centrally-placed eatery. Inexpensive.

HUNGRY TIGER: 7080 Hollywood Blvd, Hollywood, tel 462 1323. Specialist seafood restaurant. Whole Maine lobster is the speciality. Moderate.

JADE WEST: 2040 Av of the Stars, tel 556 3388. Smart Chinese restaurant located in the ABC Entertainment Center. Moderate.

JIMMY'S: 201 Moreno Dr, tel 879 2394. One of Los Angeles' top restaurants, if not the best. The décor is exquisite, and so is the food. Celebrities such as Richard Burton and Gene Kelly dine here. Expensive.

KNOLL'S BLACK FOREST INN: 124 Santa Monica Blvd, Santa Monica, tel 395 2212. Small intimate restaurant serving a good selection of German food. Cocktail lounge. Reservation advised. Moderate.

LEON'S KITCHEN & YOGURT & ICE CREAM PARLOUR: 201 N Los Angeles St, tel 613 0747. Closed Sundays and 7 pm evenings. Health food specialists. Inexpensive.

MCHENRY'S TAIL O THE COCK: 477 S La Cienaga Blvd, tel 273 1200; 12950 Ventura Blvd, N Hollywood, tel 877 0889. Two restaurants, both specialising in American cuisine. The eaterie at La Cienaga has attractive flower gardens. Moderate.

MADAME WU'S GARDEN: 2201 Wilshire Blvd, Santa Monica, tel 828 5656. Genuine Cantonese cuisine. Cocktail lounge. Moderate.

MUNICH HOFBRAU TURNER INN: 645 W 15 St, tel 747 8191. Well-known Bavarian *Bierkeller* featuring both American and European dishes. Moderate.

THE OLD SPAGHETTI FACTORY: 5939 Sunset Blvd, tel 469 7149. A very popular, individually decorated eating-house that is family owned. The pasta-based dishes are supplemented by a wide range of sauces. Children's menu. Inexpensive.

THE PALM: 9001 Santa Monica Blvd. A restaurant with sawdust on the floor, making

for a casual atmosphere. Food emphasis is on prime steaks and lobster. Expensive.

PERINO'S RESTAURANT: 4101 Wilshire Blvd, tel 383 1221. An establishment known throughout America for its international cuisine and superb service. Expensive.

PUB INN THE ALLEY: 607 S Hill St, tel 622 5794. English pub atmosphere and décor, with beer and pub meals – including Welsh Rarebit. There's even a dartboard. Closed weekends and 8 pm evenings. Inexpensive.

SCANDIA RESTAURANT: 9040 Sunset Blvd, tel 278 3555. One of the most popular restaurants in Los Angeles. Fine Scandinavian décor and specialities. Strict dress code. Expensive.

TICK TOCK RESTAURANT: 1716 N Cahuenga Blvd, tel 463 7576. Good luncheon and dinner choices in attractive surroundings. Inexpensive.

TOWER RESTAURANT: 1150 S Olive St, tel 746 1554. Central eating place way up on the 32nd storey. Moderate.

VELVET TURTLE RESTAURANT: 2255 Sawtelle Blvd, tel 477 4255. Pleasantly decorated restaurant featuring seafood entrées. Children's menu. Moderate.

THE WINDSOR RESTAURANT: 7th St at Catalina, tel 382 1261. Impressive selection of international cuisine. Expensive.

SHOPPING

ARCO PLAZA: 5th and Flower Sts. The largest underground shopping precinct in America, located beneath the Atlantic Richfield building.

BONAVENTURE SHOPPING GALLERY: 404 S Figueroa St. A plethora of diverse and expensive boutiques for the shopper with money to spare.

FARMER'S MARKET: 6333 W 3rd St. A hotchpotch of colour, crafts and food. The best of the world's produce can be found at this eye-catching market.

FISHERMAN'S VILLAGE: Marina del Rey. An interesting group of art and craft shops.

FLOWER MART: 775 S Wall St. Old-style flower stalls selling 95% of locally-grown flowers.

JAPANESE VILLA PLAZA: 350 E 1st St. Small precinct featuring every aspect of Japanese craft and ware.

PORTS O CALL VILLAGE: off Harbor Freeway, Berth 77. Rebuilt olde-worlde village with many craft shops and boutiques.

TRANSPORT

LAX INTERNATIONAL AIRPORT: 20 miles SW of Los Angeles on Century and Sepulveda Blvds. Although the airport handles 24 million passengers per year already, a new four-storey terminal has had to be constructed to cope with the predicted increase in traffic generated by the 1984 Olympic Games. There are regular links from the airport, with a choice of bus, coach or taxi. It would be wise to note, however, that taxis tend to be expensive and drivers are reluctant to make short journeys. Throughout the day car drivers can tune in (frequency 530) to special bulletins describing traffic and parking conditions in the area. Other airports in the Los Angeles district are Burbank-Glendale-Pasadena Airport, 14 miles NW; Long Beach Airport, 22 miles S; John Wayne Orange County Airport, 30 miles SE.

CAR HIRE: Rates range from $38 per day (luxury cars) down to $5 a day plus 10c a mile (economy cars). The following companies serve Los Angeles and the surrounding area: Airways, 6151 W 98th St, tel 670 8151; Avis, 1207 W 3rd St, tel 481 2000; Budget, 9775 Airport Blvd, tel 645 4500; Dollar, 6141 W Century Blvd, tel 645 9333; Hertz, 643 S Vermont Av, tel 385 7151; National, 21 World Way, tel 670 4950.

TAXIS: Because Los Angeles is such a sprawling city, fares can prove expensive. Major operators in the downtown area are: A & W, tel 466 0328;

United Independent, tel 653 5050; Independent, tel 385 8294; Checker, tel 258 3231. Red and White, tel 654 8400; Yellow, tel 670 1234 or 652 5111.

BUSES: Southern California Rapid Transit District (RTD) operates both local and express routes. For information, tel 626 4455. As the car is by far the most popular form of transport in Los Angeles the bus network is not highly developed, consequently long waits may occur when changing buses. However, there is a frequent minibus service (at 10-minute intervals) in central Los Angeles.

ORGANISED BUS TOURS: Several companies run sightseeing coach tours in and around Los Angeles. Two of the better known firms are: Gray Line Tours, 1207 W 3rd St, tel 481 8400; Starline Sightseeing Tours, 6845 Hollywood Blvd, tel 463 3131. Others are listed in the Yellow Pages of the telephone directory.

PARKING: Daytime street parking is prohibited. Many parking lots at around 80c an hour or $3 per day.

AMTRAK: Special coastline train journeys from Los Angeles to San Francisco are operated by the American passenger train service, and gamblers might like to ride the 'Desert Wind' to Las Vegas. The 'Flagstaff' takes visitors, via a bus connection, to the Grand Canyon. A USA rail pass is economically advisable for long-distance travel.

PLACES TO SEE

DISNEYLAND: 1313 Harbor Blvd, Anaheim. Huge pleasure complex transporting children and adults alike into the realms of fantasy, (see page 40).

KNOTT'S BERRY FARM: 8039 Beach Blvd, Buena Park 20 miles SE of downtown Los Angeles. A large farm with three theme areas – Old West Ghost Town, Fiesta Village and Roaring Twenties Old Time Adventures.

RANCHO LOS ALAMITOS: 6400 E Bixby Hill Rd, tel 431 2511. An 1806 adobe structure, one of the oldest in California. Furnishings are late 19th-century. Blacksmith shop.

SIX FLAGS MAGIC MOUNTAIN: off Golden State Freeway at 26101 Magic Mountain Pkwy, Valencia. 200-acre recreation and entertainment grounds. Huge roller-coasters, craft demonstrations, restaurants, snack-bars and live music.

TOURING INFORMATION

There are many visitor centres and offices in the Los Angeles district. Three of the better known organisations are: AAA, 2601 S Figueroa St (at Adams Blvd), tel 741 3111; Southern California Visitors Council, 705 W 7th St, tel 628 3101; Visitor and Convention Bureau, 800 W Katella Av.

MUSEUMS

BOWERS MUSEUM: 2002 N Main St, Santa Ana. Charts the early history of California with Indian exhibits, paintings and regional memorabilia.

CALIFORNIA MUSEUM OF SCIENCE AND INDUSTRY: 700 State Dr, Exposition Park. A fascinating museum specialising in modern audio-visual displays. The visitor is encouraged to participate by operating various illustrative devices on mathematics, energy, agriculture, space and many other subjects. The evolution of the cinema is a special feature.

HALL OF SCIENCE: Griffith Park. Many physical science exhibits on themes such as modern meteorology and satellite-tracking.

HUNTINGTON LIBRARY, ART GALLERY AND BOTANICAL GARDENS: 1151 Oxford Rd, San Marino. The library was founded on the collection of the railway magnate Henry Huntingdon and now houses one of the world's great collections of rare books. Outstanding items are the Ellesmere manuscript copy of

The Canterbury Tales and Benjamin Franklin's autobiography in his own handwriting. In the gallery there are Constable and Gainsborough exhibits. The building complex is surrounded by beautiful trees and shrubs set into variously themed gardens.

J PAUL GETTY MUSEUM: 17985 Pacific Coast Hwy, Malibu, tel 454 6541. A building fashioned on a Roman villa houses a priceless collection of Greek and Roman antiquities, Renaissance and Baroque paintings, plus 18th-century French decorative arts.

LOMITA RAILROAD MUSEUM: 250th St and Woodward Av, Lomita. The building is an Aladdin's Cave for railway enthusiasts, housing scale models, photographs and paintings of famous engines and trains. Prize exhibits are a 1902 Baldwin engine and an all-wood 1910 Union Pacific caboose (workmen's carriage).

LOS ANGELES CHILDREN'S MUSEUM: 310 N Main St, tel 687 8800. A museum designed specifically for children, who are invited to touch and become involved with the displays. Features include 'grandma's attic', a replica city street and a paint and paste workshop.

MOVIELAND-OF-THE-AIR: at Orange County Airport, Santa Ana. Large collection of early aircraft preserved in a permanent indoor display. Over 50 aeroplanes, mainly originals.

NATURAL HISTORY MUSEUM: 900 Exposition Blvd. Extensive natural history collection. Displays include fossils, mammals, minerals and insects. Music concerts on Sundays throughout summer.

NORTON SIMON MUSEUM OF ART: 411 W Colorado Blvd, Pasadena, tel 449 6840. A 1930s-style building housing many art treasures of the Renaissance and German Expressionist eras.

PACIFIC ASIA MUSEUM: 46 N Robles Av. The building is constructed in the style of a Chinese treasure house and envelops a meditation garden. The museum's theme is depiction of art and culture of the Far East and the Pacific.

SIMON WIESENTHAL CENTER FOR HOLOCAUST STUDIES: tel 553 9036. A specialist museum graphically displaying the horrors of World War II.

SOUTHWEST MUSEUM: 234 Museum Dr, tel 221 2163. The museum charts the art and culture of the American-Indians.

PARKS AND GARDENS

DESCANSO GARDENS: 1418 Descanso Dr, La Cañada, tel 790 5571. Roses, fuchsias and no less than 100,000 camellias make these shaded gardens a horticultural delight.

GREYSTONE PARK: Loma Vista Dr, Beverly Hills. 18½-acre gardens formally divided into ponds, small woods and walkways.

GRIFFITH PARK: off Los Feliz Blvd and Riverside Dr. As well as its many recreational facilities, the 4,000-acre park contains an observatory, planetarium and zoo.

LOS ANGELES STATE AND COUNTY ARBORETUM: 301 N Baldwin Av, Arcadia, tel 446 8251. The 127-acre arboretum is both a horticultural research centre and a bird sanctuary. There are several historic buildings within the grounds, including a decorative 'Queen Anne' cottage.

ROSE HILLS MEMORIAL PARK: 3900 Workman Mill Rd, Whittier. Gorgeous Pageant of Roses garden with over 750 varieties. Other gardens and arched bridges are in delightful lakeside settings.

WILL ROGERS STATE HISTORIC PARK: 14253 Sunset Blvd. A 186-acre park including the late humorist's home.

SPORT

BASEBALL: Dodger Stadium, 1000 Elysian Park Dr (Los Angeles Dodgers), tel 224 1400.

HORSE-RACING: Santa Anita Park, W Huntingdon Dr, Arcadia. Famed for thoroughbred racing since 1934. Hollywood Park, 1050 S Prairie Av. One of the largest racecourses on the West Coast. Los Alamitos Race Course, 4961 E Katella Av, Los Alamitos. Noted for its harness racing.

ICE HOCKEY: The Forum, Prairie and Manchester Avs, Inglewood (Los Angeles Kings).

POLO: Will Rogers State Historic Park. Matches are usually every Saturday.

THEATRES & CINEMAS

ABC ENTERTAINMENT CENTER: 2000 Av of the Stars, Century City. Entertainment complex including the Shubert Theatre, two movie theatres, restaurant and bar.

THE AMPHITHEATRE: above Universal Studios, Universal City. Regular summer concerts by top performers.

EBONY SHOWCASE THEATER: 4720 Washington Blvd, tel 936 1107. The oldest, Black-owned independent theatre in the city.

GREEK THEATRE: 2700 N Vermont Av, tel 660 8400. Set in a natural amphitheatre within Griffith Park, it is the scene of many dramas, concerts and ballets throughout the summer.

HOLLYWOOD BOWL: 2301 N Highland Av, tel 876 8742. Prestigious home of the Los Angeles Philharmonic Orchestra.

JOHN ANSON FORD THEATER: 2850 Cahuenga Blvd, tel 972 7428. Under the auspices of Los Angeles County, the theatre stages dramas and musicals plus an annual Shakespeare season.

MANN'S CHINESE THEATRE: 6925 Hollywood Blvd, Hollywood. A theatre famed for its exterior as much as its interior. Many stars' hand and footprints are set in concrete on the pavement outside.

THE MUSIC CENTER: 135 N Grand Av, tel 972 7485. Taking the lead in the city's theatrical revival, the Music Center contains three separate auditoria: the Ahmanson Theatre, the Mark Taper Forum and the Dorothy Chandler Pavilion.

Grand Canyon Country
Nevada, Arizona, Utah

The Grand Canyon, Arizona, from Yavapai Point. The easily discernible rock strata represent the history of the earth, each layer a geological record of a particular period

Prior to the 1930s, Nevada had little to offer apart from its mineral wealth and, like the neighbouring states of Arizona and Utah, presented to the outside world visions of dust and desert, bare mountains and crumbling ghost towns.

But, in 1931, Nevada legalised gambling. Las Vegas and Reno led the way, and today millions crowd these cities every year, hoping for that lucky strike be it through the toss of a coin, the turn of a card or the throw of a die, which could grant them fame and fortune.

Although all its dealings are monitored with scrupulous care, through gambling and liberal marriage, divorce and tax laws, Nevada sports a *risqué* reputation, one the state does not deserve, yet does nothing to dispel.

The wealth Nevada now enjoys is reflected in the quality of its roads and services, which have made accessible the magnificent, often awe-inspiring countryside of mountains and deserts it shares with Arizona and Utah.

For any visitor to the United States to go West without taking time to view the mile-deep Grand Canyon, the strange Petrified Forest or at least one of the vast national parks of multi-coloured desert and moon-like rock formations, is to deny him or herself the chance to see some of the most impressive landscape nature has wrought on earth.

Long before Las Vegas and Reno were more than dusty desert settlements in some of the most forbidding tracts of land on earth, Nevada was a magnet for mavericks. The gleam in the eyes of the tough, footloose pioneers as they crossed the burning scrubland on the way to find their El Dorado in the West was as much due to the challenge to survive in the harsh conditions as to any hopes of striking it rich at the end of the journey.

Still, there is a relevant link between the thousands of hardy adventurers of the 19th century who took the short cut over the Sierra Nevada and the deserts to California from the East and the millions who have flooded the Las Vegas and Reno gaming casinos over the last 50 years seeking an even shorter cut to fortune.

Both were attracted by the risks. Ironically, Nevada's two celebrated fleshpots are virtually the only really perilous places left for the unsuspecting intruder in the 110,000 square miles of territory. Elsewhere, modern highways with their attendant services have taken the gamble out of visiting the world's first gambling state.

In the main, Nevada belongs to yesterday's world. It is a collection of lost cities – relics of abandoned hopes – dwarfed by the awesome, uncompromising scenery around them. Like California, with which it shares its entire eastern boundary, Nevada enjoyed a fantastic mineral boom in the 19th century, but unlike its prosperous and densely populated neighbour, the soil yielded massive deposits of silver rather than gold. The finds attracted a gigantic camp following, and led to the establishment of permanent settlements close to the most productive mining strikes. But when the seams had been exhausted, the people left, leaving the homesteads and the mine workings to the desert.

Though it is the seventh largest state in the United States, Nevada's population of 610,000 is one of the smallest. Virginia City, in the heart of the silver mining area, 23 miles south-east of Reno and 16 miles north-east of Carson City, contributes only 500 people to that total. Yet in its heyday in the 1870s, it had a population of 30,000. It boasted four banks, six churches, 110 saloons and the only working lift in use anywhere between Chicago and San Francisco. The strains of honky-tonk and country and western music still drift from the saloons, and though the money is now coming from the curious tourist, the 450 shops and bars in 'C' Street, the main 'drag', are enjoying a different kind of silver boom. Souvenir stands are everywhere, recreating with the help of old photographs the period when the Comstock Lode, one of the richest deposits of lode gold and silver ever found, gave Virginia City unequalled prosperity. Discovered in 1859, the lode attracted thousands of prospectors. Until it was exhausted in 1879, the Consolidated Virginia Mine, the most productive of the strikes along the lode, offered up more than 234 million dollars worth of ore. In one year alone, 38 million dollars worth of the blue-grey mineral was extracted.

Reputedly, some of this fortune helped to build the original city of San Francisco (the one that was destroyed by the earthquake) and contributed to the funds that helped the Union forces win the Civil War. The wealth also flowed into the pockets of the successful pioneers who built majestic homes in the town. Many of them are still in pristine condition and open to the public. One such house is The Castle, built by a mine superintendent in 1868, and known as the House of Silver Doorknobs. It has a front door made of black walnut, with two monogrammed oval glass panels above, stair rods in silver, rock crystal chandeliers made in Czechoslovakia more than 150 years ago, Italian marble fireplaces and French gold-leafed mirrors. Many of the sumptuous furnishings and fittings were brought around the Cape of Good Hope to San Francisco and then 6,500 feet up into the Sierras by mule and ox.

Another souvenir of Virginia City's boom days is Piper's Opera House on 'C' Street, where the tenor Caruso, the magician, Houdini and the actress Sarah Bernhardt were all said to have performed. Now a museum open in summer months only, it is the third playhouse on the site. Two others burnt down. One of the fires was caused by the owner himself when he was 'the better for wine'. After he overturned a lamp while counting the box office receipts, John Piper was hauled out just before the roof fell in, but he insisted on crawling back as soon as the charred remains cooled to scrape up the melted gold from the two eagles which had adorned the foyer. From the salvage he raised the funds to rebuild the theatre.

Many of Virginia City's inhabitants are writers and artists, possibly drawn to it by the influence and reputation of the *Territorial Enterprise*, Nevada's first newspaper, and the inspiration of Mark Twain, who started there as a reporter many years before he became the famous author of *Tom Sawyer* and *Huckleberry Finn*. As Samuel Clemens, he first went to the town to become a prospector, but when he failed to make a quick strike, he turned to journalism and adopted the pen name Mark Twain – a river phrase meaning 'two fathoms deep'. He left the paper in 1864.

When the Comstock Lode boom was over, Nevada fell into a depression for 20 years. Revival came at the turn of the century, when more gold was discovered at Tonopah and at Goldfield in 1902, setting off another boom that lasted until 1918. Tonopah rose from the cactus and sagebrush in the heart of Nevada, and Goldfield, lying high on one side of a broad saddle between bare, broken peaks 25 miles to the south, became the centre of one of the West's largest gold finds. Some of the abandoned mines are now being reopened.

Nevada makes a great show of its history as a Wild West frontier state, and reminders of the Gold Rush days of the 19th century go hand in hand with the gambling casinos of today

Conveniently, and coincidentally, after the Goldfield mine ran out, Nevada made gambling legal in 1931. The sensational law, introduced soon after liquor prohibition came to an end, was to transform the flagging economy of the state. Although the greatest beneficiary of the bonanza that followed was the former frontier town of Las Vegas, another concentration of casinos and late night entertainment sprang up only 30 miles north-west of Virginia City, at Reno. Close to the border of California, Reno is where many of the northern Californians go for weekends, gamble freely and perhaps take advantage of the liberal marriage and divorce laws in Nevada. Calling itself the 'biggest little city in the world' it has a population of nearly 80,000 and, like Las Vegas, never sleeps. It is a truly 24-hour city.

Reno spreads its favours widely. It takes in Sparks, a city of 32,700 people on its northern boundary, and a third of Lake Tahoe, about 40 miles to the south-west. Between them, Reno and Sparks have a population of 110,000 and cater for 10 million visitors a year. In the 18 major 'resorts' (casino and hotel complexes) top-line international entertainers head glittering shows which, in the main, provide welcome diversions from the gaming tables. The range of facilities is enormous. The MGM Grand Hotel is the world's largest casino with three theatre lounges, two cinemas, seven restaurants and 40 shops. For the energetic, there is a 50-lane bowling centre, both indoor and outdoor tennis

courts, health clubs and an outdoor pool. Since it expanded recently, the hotel has opened its 2001st guest room.

Reno, too, is where the grandson of the man who invented the first slot machine on the Barbary Coast (in San Francisco in 1895) runs the Liberty Belle saloon on South Virginia Street, and displays a unique collection of antique one-armed bandits.

In Sparks, one of the more unusual attractions away from the casinos, is Harrah's Automobile Collections. Originating in 1948 with two veteran cars, a 1911 Maxwell and a 1911 Ford, it is the world's largest novelty car 'compound' with more than 1,000 antique, vintage, classic and special interest cars on display. Among them are Al Jolson's 1933 Cadillac, Tyrone Power's 1930 Duesenberg, and a range of engines from a two-horse-power motorized jalopy

to a 2,000-horse-power dragster. Reno, of course, is not all fun and games, and is proud to support the University of Nevada, which includes a school of mines, founded in 1874, on its 193-acre campus.

Amid a profusion of pine trees and sparkling water, and against a backdrop of the peaks of the Sierra Nevada, the eastern shore of Lake Tahoe (the rest is in California) takes full advantage of the Nevada freedoms. Apart from the casinos and hotel 'resorts', the lake offers Vikingsholm, a 38-room reproduction of a 9th-century Norse fortress in Emerald Bay.

An hour's drive away from the bustle and clamour of Reno are two other lakes – the 32-mile long Pyramid Lake, with its strange rock formations, to the north-east, and Donner Lake, a water-skiing centre, to the

Carson City, the capital of Nevada

RENO

Hotels

HARRAH'S HOTEL: At Center and 2nd Sts, tel 786 3232. 325 rooms. Expensive.

HOLIDAY INN: 2 locations. Downtown; 1000 E 6th St, tel 786 5151, 300 rooms. South; 5851 S Virginia St, tel 825 2940. 151 rooms. Expensive.

Restaurants

THE BUNDOX: 1st and Lake Sts, in River House Motor Hotel, tel 323 0324. Small dining room overlooking Truckee River. Continental cuisine. Expensive.

VARIO'S: 1695 S Virginia St, tel 329 2581. Northern Italian and American dishes. Moderate-expensive.

Places of Interest

ATMOSPHERIUM AND PLANETARIUM: University of Nevada, N Virginia St. Changing shows of astronomical events past, present and future.

MINING MUSEUM: Mackay School of Mines, at University. Mining history and collections geological, metallurgical, and mineralogical.

west. On the slopes of the mountains is the largest concentration of ski facilities in the world, with over 100 major lifts at 22 locations. In these surroundings is Carson City, about 30 miles south of Reno, which became the capital of Nevada in 1864, six years after it was founded. The original Capitol building is still in use and parts are

---

CARSON CITY

Hotels

FRONTIER MOTEL: 1718 N Carson St, tel 882 1377. 50 rooms. Moderate.

THE OMSBY HOUSE: 600 S Carson St, tel 882 1890. 202 rooms. Expensive.

Restaurant

THE GOURMET TABLE: 400 S Carson St, tel 883 1510. Excellent French cuisine. Expensive.

---

open to the public. In this city of 26,000 people are signs of the wealth the Comstock Lode lavished on its exploiters. Bowers Mansion, which overlooks Washoe Lake 10 miles north of the town, cost $200,000 to build. Open to the public, the mansion has been partially restored and contains some original furnishings. In the city itself, the State Museum in the old Mint Building displays the minerals and ores which made the state wealthy.

Just south of Carson City is Genoa, founded by a trader sent by Brigham Young, the Mormon leader. This was the first permanent settlement in Nevada, and a two-acre site is devoted to the Mormon Station Historic State Monument. Here is a replica of a log stockade and trading post, which was the site of the first territorial government of Nevada.

Nearly 100 miles north-east of Reno lies Lovelock, on the edge of the Forty-Mile Desert. It is appropriately named, having cornered some of Nevada's fast marriage and divorce market. Not that the man it is named after ever had such 20th-century ideas. George Lovelock owned a ranch where the town now stands. Countless Forty-Niners (the name for the prospectors who joined the Californian gold rush of 1849), and thousands of horses and oxen perished in the region before reaching their ultimate goal. Lovelock today is covered in modern highways and grows a delicious species of melon. In fact, Nevada's largest farming district is 40 miles south at Fallon. Site of the Fallon United States Naval Air Station, it is also one of the best-stocked duck-hunting grounds, and a centre for prize turkey breeding.

Gabbs, about 50 miles further south-east, is the nearest 'living' town to the Berlin-Ichthyosaur State Park – 903 acres of rock and woodlands containing the fossilised remains of huge aquatic reptiles. These prehistoric creatures existed 180 million years ago when Nevada was covered by a warm sea; some weighed as much as 30 tons and grew up to 70 feet long. Berlin itself, unlike its famous European namesake, sur-

vived as a town for only 13 years. It was founded in 1897 and was left to the desert in 1910, a crumbling epitaph to a get-rich-quick society. In its fleeting heyday, it had a general store, an assay office, a stagecoach station, a barber's shop, numerous homes and boarding houses, a log-built schoolhouse and three saloons. It also supported about 300 people – a doctor, nurse, nightwatchman, forest ranger, postmaster, 13 housewives, 12 schoolchildren, one Chinese cook called Chinee Joe, one prostitute and 207 miners! The small cemetery below the town marks the graves of some of the pioneers who died from the hardships of life in those early mining days.

Near the eastern boundaries of Nevada, the Humboldt National Forest covers 2.5 million acres, scattered along several of the mountain ranges that lie in giant strips running vertically across the central portion of the state. Here, too, are the sites of several ghost towns.

Ely's population of 6,000 administers the tourist attractions of Hamilton, 45 miles

---

ELY

Hotel

GRAND CENTRAL MOTEL: 15th and Lyons Av, tel 289 4406. 13 rooms. Moderate.

---

west, and preserves what remains of the profitable years in the 1860s when the town produced more than nine million dollars worth of silver ore. So much silver was found that it paid for most of the Civil War debts. A monument to those days are the six stone beehive charcoal ovens, each over 30-foot tall, which provided charcoal for the smelt workers. Hundreds of men were employed to cut the pine trees from the surrounding hills, and haul them by oxen to the ovens for use as fuel. Eventually, due to neglect, the sagebrush grew over the ovens and almost obliterated them. They have only recently been reclaimed.

Another ghost town, Treasure City, three miles south of Hamilton, produced three million dollars from a single 70 by 40 by 30-foot hole. Yet another is Cherry Creek, 45 miles north of Ely, and it still enjoys some mining activities. At Osceola, 40 miles east of Ely, a 25lb gold nugget was found. Also in this area, five miles west of Baker on the Arizona border is a treasure of another kind. The Lehman caves at the foot of Wheeler Peak are illuminated marble caverns displaying remarkable and colourful rock formations. The visitor centre tells how the caves were formed.

One of the most famous ghost towns stands about two and a half miles west of Beatty, in the south-west of Nevada.

Brigham Young's statue in Salt Lake City, the Mormon who led the colonisation of Utah

Left: Hopi Indians of the Grand Canyon performing the Eagle Dance

Below: A house built of bottles in Rhyolite, a once booming mining town

Rhyolite had 12,000 inhabitants in 1907, but like so many communities that fell on hard times when the mines were exhausted it has been virtually deserted for nearly half a century. Today, a railway depot, stone and steel building ruins, and an interesting house constructed of bottles are reminders of Rhyolite's glory.

The precursor of Nevada's lost cities is enshrined in the Lost City Museum at Overton, about 50 miles north-east of Las Vegas. Overton was once a great metropolis of about 15,000 inhabitants, inheriting an Indian culture that was one of the highest of all the Indian tribes in the United States. They lived in ornate and well-equipped pueblos, extending for 30 miles on both sides of what was then the Muddy River, but is now more decorously called the Virgin River. In the museum are remains of a people who lived 1,500 years ago. Other tribes, including the Hopi, took over the 'amenities', the last being the Paiute, who followed in AD 1100 and whose descendants, like the Hopis, still live in Nevada. The city itself was probably abandoned between AD 800 and AD 900, its citizens migrating to north-east Arizona and parts of Utah.

Today, Arizona and Utah are home to most of the Indian tribes. About a fifth of America's Indian population still live on reservations. One in 20 of Arizona's 2,270,000 population – that's more than 100,000 people – are Indians, representing a seventh of the entire Indian population in the United States. The 19 Indian reservations take up a quarter of the state's 114,000 square miles. The Navajo reservation, which covers over 25,000 square miles of canyons, forested mountains, and desert, is the largest in the United States, and many other ancient and noble tribes, with names as romantic as the stories author Zane Grey immortalized them in, have survived bloody wars, disease and the white man's domination. Though tourists can visit many of their hard-won territories, many of the reservations are usually isolated and often even inaccessible to the stranger unaccustomed to the terrain. They do provide, however, fascinating glimpses into a fast vanishing culture. The Indians value their privacy and are usually not keen to be photographed.

The Havasupai, though a small tribe of farmers and stockmen, are of particular interest to the tourist, because for hundreds of years they have inhabited the isolated canyon of Havasu Creek in the western part of the Grand Canyon. Unfortunately, their idyllic home can only be reached down a

THE BOTTLE HOUSE BUILT IN 1905 OF SOME 50000 BEER BOTTLES BY A TOM KELLY FROM BOTTLES COLLECTED FROM LOCAL SALOONS 3 ROOMS YOU ARE WELCOME TO COME IN AND BROWSE SOUVENIRS FOR SALE

steep 8-mile trail. They can be encountered, however, selling beads and trinkets at many tourist locations in the Grand Canyon National Park.

GRAND CANYON NATIONAL PARK

Hotels

GRAND CANYON LODGE: at North Rim, tel 638 2611. 215 rooms. Moderate.

RED FEATHER LODGE: 9 miles S of Grand Canyon Village, tel 638 2673. 130 rooms. Moderate.

Places of Interest

GRAND CANYON: one of the world's most outstanding natural spectacles. There is a free mini-bus service along West Rim Drive and around the village area during the summer months. Various other tours and bicycle hire are also available.

VISITOR CENTER: One mile E of Grand Canyon Village. General information, maps and ranger guidance, plus museum.

WATCHTOWER: Desert View, 25 miles E of Grand Canyon Village. Located on the edge of the canyon wall, the tower commands views of the river, canyon, Painted Forest and the Kaibab National Forest.

One of the greatest wonders in the world, the Grand Canyon provides 277 miles of awesome spectacle – especially dramatic when seen from the air. The Colorado River, for six million years the architect of this phenomenon, has eaten away 500,000

tons of sand and lime every day, but since the Glen Canyon Dam 100 miles upstream was finished in 1963, the river's insatiable appetite has been reduced to 80,000 tons a day. Flowing at an average speed of 12 miles an hour, the Colorado has cleaved through the Canyon, opening up a gorge 18 miles wide at one point and only 300 feet wide at another. There is a quarter of a mile difference in the height of the two rims of the Canyon, creating spectacular variations in weather and temperature.

The first recorded sighting of the Canyon by a white man was in 1540, when a member of an expedition in search of the Seven Golden Cities of Cibola first set eyes on it. It was to be another 317 years before it was sighted again. A Lieutenant Ives describes it in his log as a 'profitless place' he would never want to visit again. But 12 years later sufficient interest was aroused in these reports for Major John Wesley Powell to lead the first expedition to explore the length of the Canyon. While one needs to be fit and well-equipped to tackle the Canyon trails which the Havasupais originally carved out of the slopes to build their dwellings, the animal and plant life the canyon holds are considerable compensation for the effort involved. About 70 species of mammals, 250 species of bird, 25 types of reptiles and five sorts of amphibious creatures are known to inhabit the region. Another way to negotiate the slopes is on muleback, but visitors weighing over 16 stone, children under 12, the handicapped, pregnant women and visitors un-

One of the world's outstanding spectacles, the Grand Canyon, through which the Colorado River has flowed for six million years, gradually cutting deeper and deeper into the earth's crust. The canyon plunges 5,700 feet at its deepest point

able to speak fluent English are barred.

The Colorado River, having fashioned a natural miracle, inspired man to try and follow suit. He created Hoover Dam – one of the seven engineering marvels of America – to tame the power of the river and prevent persistent flooding. The dam was made operational in 1935, and the 726-foot-high horseshoe-shaped wall of concrete, 660-foot thick at the base, irrigates much of Arizona, Southern Nevada and Southern California (see page 63). It has also spawned one of the largest artificial lakes in the Western hemisphere – the 115-mile-long Lake Mead, which stores the means for hydro-electric power and irrigation. It is also a major tourist attraction, and on its 550-mile shoreline there are six large recreational centres.

To the north of the lake is the Valley of Fire State Park. The winding passages leading through the 30,000 acres of red sandstone are easy to get lost in, and it is wise to stay on marked trails to see the ancient petroglyphs (picture-writing in rock), some showing dragons drawn thousands of years ago. It has also been 'immortalized' numerous times by Hollywood, as it is a favourite location for the filming of Westerns.

The Mormon Monument, Salt Lake City, where Brigham Young first saw Salt Lake Valley

The capital of Arizona is Phoenix, the heart of the state. Here the cowboy and the New York businessman are equally at home in a brash but sophisticated city that owes its successful growth to the completion of

Petroglyphs, or rock carvings, made by the ancestors of today's Indians thousands of years ago, found in the Valley of Fire

the Roosevelt Dam on the Salt River in 1911 (which provided irrigation and power for industry), and the arrival of the Southern Pacific Railroad in 1926. The first European to settle here was John Smith, who established a hay camp in 1864 to supply forage to a nearby army post at Camp MacDowell, but the earliest inhabitants were the Hohokam Indians, who conquered the desert with a system of irrigation ditches, long before the white man, but whose civilisation mysteriously disappeared around 1450. Today, this thriving capital is a sprawl of countless suburbs, shopping centres and ranch-style homes, coloured by the Spanish colonial and Indian pueblo architecture. Only 100 years ago Phoenix was an archetypal lawless wild-west frontier town of saloons, gambling palaces, rowdy cowboys, soldiers and ever-hopeful miners.

The most notable museum in the city is the Heard Museum, which is devoted to Arizona's anthropology, history and Indian art. The Desert Botanical Garden is a museum of rather a different kind, where 150 acres of the city's Papago Park is turned over to the different species of plants found in the deserts of the world. The height of the blooming season is late March to April. In contrast are the islands and lagoons of green and lush Encanto Park, which serves as a waterfowl refuge and where the many unusual trees and shrubs make a welcome change to the arid and brown desert of the surrounding countryside.

In the south of the state, in a high desert

valley which was once the floor of an ancient sea, is Tucson, one of the oldest Spanish settlements in the American west. The area was first visited by Eusebio Francisco Kino in 1692, but was not settled until 1776. During the 1800s, however, gold was discovered, and Tucson became a mining town. There are tours available to several nearby ghost towns left behind after the gold rush.

In Tucson Mountain Park, in 30,000 acres of the Tucson Mountains, is the Arizona-Sonora Desert Museum, where local plant and animal life can be seen at close quarters. Also in the museum are underground cave galleries, which show subterranean life and geology. The Arizona State Museum, on the University of Arizona campus (the university was founded in 1885), contains the most comprehensive collections of American south-western archaeology in existence, and includes stone sculptures carved over 10,000 years ago. Rather more recent history is explained at the Mission San Xavier Del Bac, in the Papago Indian Reservation nine miles south-west of the city. This is a beautiful example of Spanish mission architecture – the domes, carvings, arches and flying buttresses of the 'White Dove of the Desert' are superior to any other of the 18th-century missions, and appear almost to have been inspired by the glorious natural architecture of the deserts and mountains.

Utah's most spectacular development was in the 19th century, due largely to the Mormons. These hard-working religious pioneers, inspired by their famous second leader, Brigham Young, founded Salt Lake City on 24 July 1847. Earning its name because of its proximity to the Great Salt Lake on its north-west boundary, it became the capital of the Mormon community and

later of the state. It now has a population of 168,700. The lake, with the exception of the Dead Sea, is the saltiest body of water on earth and can buoy up a human body.

Industrious and dedicated to the point of being fanatical, the Mormons introduced all kinds of astonishingly progressive work practices. They dammed a creek and developed what is thought to be the first irrigation method used by American whites. Though only a handful of Mormons at first settled in Salt Lake City, Brigham Young soon found plenty of volunteers, in the wake of the first discovery of iron deposits in southern Utah, to send to the Iron Mission in Cedar City nearly 250 miles south. In 1850, they colonised the area, and within 10 months, produced a rich output

another industrial problem – the production of cotton. St George had a freakish semi-tropical climate – ideal for cotton growing. In their customarily efficient way, the Mormons established a Cotton Mission to produce supplies of fibre during the Civil War, and soon made St George the centre of the cotton-growing industry in Utah. St George is named after Brigham Young's right-hand man, George H A Swift, who helped to found the city. Here, too, was where they built their first Mormon Temple in Utah in 1869. It still stands with several other early buildings, as does Brigham Young's winter home, which is open to visitors.

Brigham City is named after him and lies about 50 miles north of Salt Lake City. Apart from having several mementoes from the early days of the Mormon settlement, this city of 14,000 people has the 64,000-acre Migratory Bird Refuge on marshes that in autumn become host to 20,000 whistling swans and half a million ducks.

Rivalling the Grand Canyon in many ways, Bryce Canyon National Park and Zion National Park provide spectacles of breathtaking magnitude and splendour. At Bryce, a series of horseshoe-shaped amphitheatres have been carved out of some of the most colourful rocks on the earth's crust.

---

of iron, establishing Cedar Fort as a foundry for iron mining and manufacturing. Indian opposition, floods, and faults in the furnaces eventually led to the foundry being closed in 1858. Today, however, the legacy of their labours can be inspected at the Iron Mission State Historical Monument in Cedar City which, with its population of 10,700, still operates a flourishing open-pit iron-ore mining industry.

The city has an annual Shakespearian Festival in July and August, presented by the Southern Utah Stage College. Lively Elizabethan dancing, lute playing and singing conjure up the seventeenth-century English atmosphere. Alta, a ski resort about 30 miles south-east of the city, provides other diversions for the tourist.

In October 1861, 308 indefatigable Mormons moved another 50 miles south almost to the Arizona border. They were called by Brigham Young to St George to tackle

The Temple of Osiris is one of several mighty sculptures in this 36,007-acre park.

In the 147,000 acres of Zion National Park, the Zion Canyon, half a mile deep and a mile wide, has been cut by the Virgin River. Dominated by two gigantic stone masses – the 2,500-foot-high Watchman, and the 7,795-foot-high West Temple the park is a myriad-hued land of sandstone, shale and limestone.

Among the other national parks in Utah which display the magnificent scenery of the state is the Arches National Monument, five miles north-west of Moab, where erosion has carved holes in the bare red rock, some so large that they have become arches or natural bridges – Landscape Arch, in the Devil's Garden, has a span of 291 feet and a height of 105 feet. Even more spectacular is the multi-coloured Rainbow Bridge in the Rainbow Bridge National Monument just north of the Arizona-Utah border. This almost perfectly formed arch stretches 278 feet, 290 feet above the stream which helped to create it. Two other spectacular parks are Canyonlands, 337,258 acres around the confluence of the Green and Coloradao rivers, renowned for its colourful rock spires, and Capitol Reef, where exposed rock beds give a graphic insight into the way the earth's surface is constructed.

The Glen Canyon National Recreation Area, which stretches from north-central Arizona into Utah, surrounds Lake Powell. The lake winds through towering red cliffs and its blue waters fill hundreds of secret coves, inlets and canyons, resulting in a constantly changing shoreline longer than the entire US west coast. Sandy beaches, waterskiing, boating and fishing are unexpected pleasures the lake offers in this desert land of the mid-west. Raft trips along the San. Juan River, which flows into the lake, are available from Mexican Hat.

MEXICAN HAT

Hotel

SAN JUAN HOTEL: Monument Valley off US 163, tel 683 2220. 22 rooms. Inexpensive.

Relics of prehistoric times can be found at the Dinosaur Quarry Visitor Center, seven miles north of Jensen, which is part of the Dinosaur National Monument. Here is one of the world's largest concentrations of fossilised remains. The silicified bones of many kinds of dinosaurs and prehistoric reptiles can be seen in a permanent exhibition on one of the quarry faces, where they have been uncovered but otherwise left as they were found. Visitors can watch technicians as they unearth the fossilised skeletal remains. This is a fitting visit to pair with a tour of Arizona's Petrified Forest National Park, where fossilised trees 200 million years old lie in a jumble on the ground just as they were deposited by the prehistoric streams which swept them down from the mountains. As in many of the region's rock formations, the various ores of the earth have stained the trees brilliant colours. Points of interest in the park include Agate Bridge, which is a petrified log spanning a 40-foot chasm – 111 feet of the ancient tree are exposed – and the Rainbow Forest Museum at the entrance to the park, where there are exhibits of objects found in the forest, and which explains how the trees came to be here.

These natural phenomena and extraordinary landscapes are unquestionably the great attractions these states have to offer the tourist – there can be few of nature's wonders which leave a more distinct and lasting impression.

The fantastic rock formations carved out of the earth's crust by erosion found in the Bryce Canyon National Park, which covers 36,007 acres

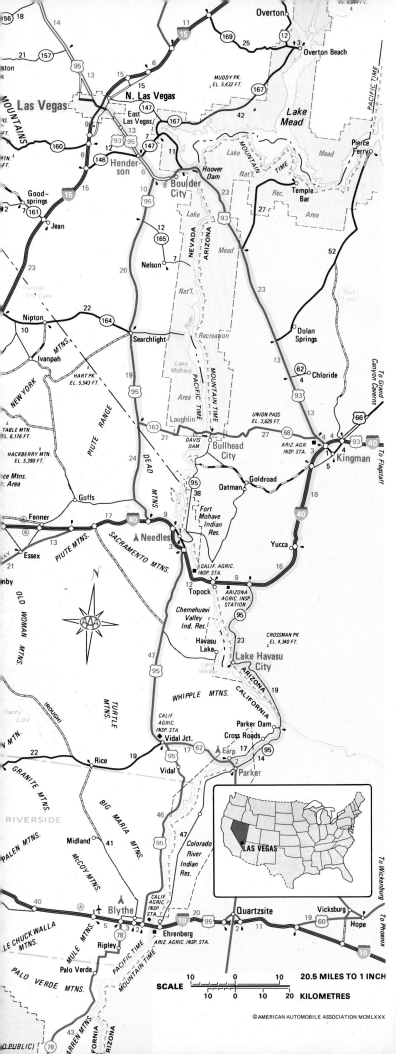

Hoover Dam and Lake Havasu

2–3 days – 372 miles

Las Vegas – Lake Mohave – Lake Havasu City – Kingman – Lake Mead and the Hoover Dam – Henderson – Las Vegas

Leave Las Vegas on US 95 and continue for 55 miles then take an unclassified road to Lake Mohave.

Lake Mohave

A popular leisure resort and a fisherman's paradise, Lake Mohave extends southwards from the hub of the Hoover Dam. The lake's cold waters are drawn from the depths of its sister, Lake Mead, and nearby Willow Beach National Fish Hatchery supplies the fish, mainly trout. Popular year-round pastimes on Lake Mohave are sailing, swimming and water-skiing. Caravan sites and other accomodation are located nearby.

Return to US 95 and proceed for 40 miles beyond Searchlight, a once thriving mining centre, then turn off onto Interstate 40 to pass Needles and rejoin the southbound US 95 in 12 miles. Drive 40 miles then join State Route 62 at Vidal Junction. Travel for 12 miles to Parker and join State Route 95 proceeding northwards for Lake Havasu and passing Buckskin Mountain/Colorado River State Park.

Lake Havasu City and Lake Havasu

A relative newcomer to the Chemehuevi Valley, Lake Havasu City was founded in 1964 as a speculative venture. It is now a popular resort centre for Lake Havasu which was formed by the building of the Parker Dam. The dam is situated just south of the city on State Route 95. London visitors may be particularly surprised by one of the main attractions here – the London Bridge. Its granite elegance now spans a channel of the Colorado River. Now the proud possession of the McCulloch Corporation, the bridge was sold to them in 1969 when London authorities decided maintenance was too expensive. Its sale fetched nearly $2\frac{1}{2}$ million dollars; $60,000 more than the agreed price. The difference was a sentimental gesture on behalf of the chairman of the McCulloch Corporation and represented his age in thousands. The historic bridge, designed by John Rennie in 1831, was dismantled and the 10,000 tons of granite transported to Arizona where it was re-erected

piece by piece in the desert. Part of the river was re-routed by means of a specially-excavated channel, to allow water to flow under the bridge in a realistic manner. It cost 5 million dollars to ship the bridge from London to the USA. To complete the scene, an English 'village' with London bus, taxi and pub stands alongside the bridge, and a recording of the chimes of Big Ben booms out every hour.

The Indians knew this place long before it became one of Arizona's leading holiday spots, and they named it 'havasu' which means 'land of the blue-green water'. This water is a great attraction to the fisherman as well as the

LAKE HAVASU CITY

Hotels

BEST WESTERN WINGS MOTOR HOTEL: 33 Pima Dr, tel 855 2146. 40 rooms. Moderate.

HOLIDAY INN: 271 Lake Havasu Av S, tel 855 1111. 200 rooms. Expensive.

SANDMAN INN: 1700 McCulloch Blvd, tel 855 7841. 91 rooms. Moderate.

Restaurant

LE TRIANON HENRIS: 34 Scott St, tel 855 4667. A small, elegantly decorated restaurant serving French cuisine. Expensive.

sightseer – the picturesque shoreline of this beautiful lake is more than 45 miles long. Agate, jasper and turquoise are plentiful in the surrounding rocky red cliffs. Eight miles north of the city is Topock Gorge; part of Havasu National Wildlife Refuge, it can be reached by boat tour from the marina or by means of a footpath. The gorge shelters many species of birds – herons, loons, falcons and cormorants, and a most sought-after inhabitant – the Harris Hawk, one of the country's rarest birds of prey. Apart from the spectacular scenery, the gorge is also famous for its petroglyphs – fascinating rock carvings incised by the original Indian inhabitants in ancient times.

Leave Lake Havasu City on State Route 95 and continue for 23 miles to the Mohave Mountains exit and take Interstate 40 into Kingman.

Lake Havasu, the 46-mile-long lake created by the Parker Dam and fed by the mighty Colorado River

Kingman

400 West Beale Street is the site of the Mohave Museum of History and Arts whose exhibits trace the history and development of north-west Arizona.

KINGMAN

Hotels

BEST WESTERN WAYFARER'S INN: 2815 E Andy Devine, tel 753 6271. 100 rooms. Moderate.

RAMADA INN: 1400 E Andy Devine, tel 753 5531. 100 rooms. Expensive.

RANCHITO MOTEL: 2803 E Andy Devine, tel 753 2935. 15 rooms. Inexpensive.

Leave Kingman on US 93 and drive through rocky country and desert for 70 miles to Lake Mead.

Lake Mead and the Hoover Dam

At over 115-miles long, Lake Mead is one of the largest man-made lakes in the world. It has the capacity for storing two years' flow from the river and this water provides hydro-electric power, irrigation for the parched desert lands of south-west America and Mexico, and a water supply to many cities in Nevada and California. Dry, sandy mountains rise steeply from the lake shore and many tracks lead through fine walking country, which is best appreciated in the cooler months. The Sierra Madre is home to the puma, deer, mountain sheep, wild ass and the golden eagle, and, in springtime, wild flowers grace the hillsides. On the west side of the lake, at Boulder Beach, there is safe bathing, camping and restaurant facilities. Boat tours leave from Lake Mead Maria, north of Boulder Beach.

The massive Hoover Dam, one of America's seven wonders of civil engineering, was built in the 1930s to protect the surrounding countryside from the disastrous flooding of the Colorado River, which frequently burst its banks and sent a raging torrent 14,000 miles down the Rocky Mountains to the Pacific. Built in a horseshoe shape, the dam wall measures a gargantuan 726 feet high and 660-feet thick, tapering to a mere 45 feet at the crest. It cost a tidy 175 million dollars when it was completed in 1935.

During the dam's construction, Boulder City was built to house the workers. Nowadays it is a thriving tourist centre selling crafts such as pottery, leatherware and

Mexican goods. Originally Boulder Dam, Hoover Dam was re-named in honour of Herbert J Hoover who was President of the United States at that time. Black Canyon is a good vantage point from which to view the dam; there are parking places on both sides. For those who want a closer inspection, there are guided tours of the dam at frequent intervals throughout the day. Visitors are taken almost to river level by lift and then inside through part of the complex system of tunnels which were bored into the cliffs to house the massive generators. Models of the generators and the course of the Colorado River can be found in the Exhibition Building, along with an explanation of the history and workings of the dam.

From the Hoover Dam take US 93 and continue for 18 miles to Henderson.

Henderson

Old Vegas, situated on Boulder Highway, is an entertainment centre that re-lives the heyday of the American West. An old army fort and antique steam trains are on show and a cast of Western characters act out roles, gunfights and such like, for the amusement of the audience. Nevada's history is the subject of an interesting filmshow.

Continue on US 93 for 16 miles back to Las Vegas.

A view from the top of the Hoover Dam, looking down Black Canyon. The dam was built to control the disastrous floods caused by the Colorado River when swollen with the melting snows from its source in the Rocky Mountains. Huge turbines in the dam provide hydro-electric power

Las Vegas

In the midst of a sparse and arid desert, surrounded by treeless mountains, lies a boom town that's still booming – Las Vegas. Burnt by fierce sun by day, lit by the glare of neon at night, this tinsel city never sleeps.

Las Vegas is gambling. Stakes start from as low as a nickel, and rise to $5,000 in the chandeliered and panelled casinos. The finest entertainers in the world come here to perform. You can dine while watching a circus perform above you, or play tennis at four o'clock in the morning, or eat breakfast at any time of the day or night you choose.

Everything in Las Vegas is for fun. Everything is bigger – a hot dog's 'a yard long', a beefburger 'a prime two pounder' – and there is something for everyone.

There is little to remind you of the past in 'Vegas'. It's a contemporary town.

There are few clocks, the time of day means little in this non-stop city. You can even get married, at any hour, at a neon-advertised wedding chapel – it takes fifteen minutes – or if it takes your fancy, have the ceremony performed underwater or in a helicopter.

In Las Vegas, you can do anything for money.

Surrounded by arid wastes of desert and mountains, Las Vegas should have no more substance than a mirage on the horizon. Instead, in one of the loneliest areas in America, where only six people share every square mile, this glittering jewel has become an oasis dedicated to the pursuit of pleasure, money, and making dreams come true.

From the air, the city looks fabulous – a kind of Atlantis of the desert, and to arrive in Las Vegas is to be confronted by a wall of neon lights burning into the desert sky, and house-high hoardings beckoning promises of such extravagant delights that they contribute to the sense of unreality and fantasy.

A tinselled world of glamour and extravagance, Las Vegas is where money can be made and lost more quickly and in more ways than almost anywhere else. Gambling – or gaming, to use the word preferred by the Las Vegas casinos – has brought the city and state riches beyond their wildest expectations. In 1931, after several decades of economic decline following the end of the gold and silver rushes of the last 100 years, Nevada became the first state in America to legalise gambling – thereby exposing Las Vegas to a new kind of strike-it-rich frenzy. Since then, the city and its rival gambling, marriage and divorce counterpart, Reno, have cornered the market in the fast-buck business.

Las Vegas has come a long way since the turn of the century when the population consisted of five lawyers, three doctors, two dentists, one plumber and eleven saloon keepers. It took 40 years for the first hotel casino at the junction of Sahara Avenue and Las Vegas Boulevard (known as the Strip) to be opened. Now there are more than 40 major hotels in and around the Strip, the city's main artery. More than 12 million people a year converge on this five-mile stretch of Interstate 15, which links Las Vegas with Salt Lake City nearly 500 miles in the north, and with Los Angeles on the Californian coast 400 miles to the west. Las Vegas earns a staggering billion and a half dollars a year.

There are at least nine ways to win or lose money at the toss of a coin, the throw of a dice or the turn of a card. All of them can be played in the softly-lit and

Gambling is the life-blood of Las Vegas, and it dominates the town day and night – even art is not excused, as shown by this dice montage (inset)

65

velvety-plush surroundings of the gaming rooms. These alluring, windowless places all look the same. Shut off from reality as one is in such an environment, it is sometimes difficult to remember where one is, what time it is, even what day (or night) it is. There are no clocks in the gaming rooms, no public clocks in the streets and, unlike London, no reassuring policemen pounding the beat to stop and ask the time. Time, in a sense, doesn't exist in Las Vegas, and in the tense atmosphere of a casino it is somewhat irrelevant.

Appropriately, Las Vegas has what its owner, an ex-bookmaker, claims is the largest gamblers' bookshop in the world. Since he opened the business in 1970, John Luckman has built up a stock of 1,000 gambling titles, despatching £250,000 worth a year from his store at 630 S 11th St all over the world.

Even food takes second place in many people's list of priorities. Though it is possible to eat well in Las Vegas (see Directory) comparatively few people make time for it. Many resorts provide quick-service meals with gigantic portions (enough to satisfy the appetite of many Europeans for a whole day) at absurdly low cost. A typical example is at the Circus Circus Hotel where breakfast consists of a choice of a score or more dishes. You can take as much as you want from each, and even return to the queue at the self-service counter for more. It costs about the equivalent of two portions of fish and chips. Such is the gambling fever in the city that nearly every supermarket, restaurant and hotel bar has the ubiquitous phalanx of one-armed bandits lurking just inside the door.

Las Vegas has another enormously profitable side to its numerous fun palaces: the shows. The city deserves its high reputation for attracting the world's foremost entertainers and paying them astronomical salaries for the privilege of performing in front of 30,000 tourists every night. Dazzling shows, some costing hundreds of thousands of dollars are staged in huge cocktail-lounge theatres. Instead of tip-up seats, they are equipped with tiered tables, the majority set at right angles to the stage. At Caesars Palace, the Circus Maximus can seat 1,300 people for a glamorous spectacular staged twice nightly. The late show is usually more popular and often does not start until after midnight. Very often the audience has to be in position up to an hour and a half before the performance starts. The regular patron gets there even earlier if he wants to make sure that, suitably tipped with what is euphemistically called 'folding favour', the waiter or the maitre D (for d'hotel) finds him a strategic seat. Once slotted into his place at a canteen-style table, he may only ever see that portion of the stage which is in his direct line of vision. To turn round is often a complicated manoeuvre involving the connivance of people on each side. No meals are provided, but the drinks arrive in a flurry of activity over the heads of the audience, carried by attendants performing great balancing feats between the tables. Two drinks for each guest is normal practice. Once the show starts no more drinks are served.

The wedding chapels are another notorious Las Vegas convention. Dressed in garish neon, they offer a service no less enthusiastic than the hotel resorts next door. At the last count there were 30 of them – mostly on the Strip – with evocative names like Cupid's Wedding Chapel, Silver Bells, Wee Kirk

O' the Heather, and Hitching Post. At the Circus Circus Hotel the 'Chapel of the Fountain' offers instant bliss in sepulchral surroundings, with organ music, a cassette recording of the event, the choice of ribbons, and the licence fee costing about £50. A 'Marrying Sam', (the nickname of the officiating minister), and a recording of the Wedding March come free! Every year more than 50,000 couples come to Las Vegas to take this bizarre road up the aisle, although quite a few come back for a divorce.

Circus Circus Hotel is the embodiment of the spirit of Las Vegas and, unlike most hotels, it even provides entertainment for children in a city where nearly everything panders to adult tastes. As its name implies, Circus Circus looks like a Big Top. Acrobats

▶ *Wedding chapels offering instant marriages with all the trimmings are one of the more surprising products of Nevada's liberal laws*

▼ *Las Vegas touts for business unashamedly, advertisements vie for attention using every inducement to attract custom, creating a uniquely colourful townscape*

photographer with a fancy-dress wardrobe which can transform his sitters into anything from Wyatt Earp to Mae West.

Free is the most overused four-letter word in Las Vegas. Some of the hotels make extravagant offers, particularly on hoardings: 'Free $277 gambling certificate'. 'Free breakfast including champagne. Free dinners. Free old-fashioned foot-long hot dogs. Free cocktails. Free guaranteed slot wins.' You can even have 'breakfast 24-hours round the clock, with free room and colour adult movie'. Such generosity is not misplaced. The more they can give away, the more the visitor spends at the tables or in the fruit machines.

Las Vegas, however, is not a city of sin and debauchery. Like the state, it keeps a very tight grip on the many facets of its own attractions, and though its history is short its reputation for keeping orderly house is unsullied. It has also put some of the vast fortunes from its gambling activities to good community use. Taxes are lower and school places more plentiful than in many American cities of similar size and standing. There are about 200 churches, and most of the half million people who live there are fiercely proud of the city's cultural, social and religious influences. Ballet and dance performances are often staged with the help of the professional showgirls who front the major spectaculars on the Strip. The Nevada Dance Theater has its home at the 600-seater Judy Bayley Theater in the grounds of the University of Nevada.

The 300-acre campus is just a few minutes drive from the Strip, an incongruous academic bastion which has on its premises the Artemus Ham Concert Hall where 2,000 people at a time can hear world-famous musicians like Aaron Copeland, Isaac Stern and Eugene Ormandy perform with distinguished visiting orchestras. Since it was founded in 1957, the university has made room for 9,000 students. Here, too, is to be found the Museum of Natural History

▼ Showgirls add to the glamour and glitter of Las Vegas' nightspots, which attract America's top entertainers

swing on trapezes from the roof virtually over the heads of the casino punters who hardly spare a glance at the upstairs arena. The performances are free, frequent and first-class. Even the sideshows, so important to the atmosphere of a circus when it comes to town, are authentic, although the shops for adults in the downstairs corridors are not much more sophisticated. Very popular, for instance, is a novelty

where Indian artefacts and a thousand-piece mineral collection from all over the world are on show.

The Juanita Greer White Hall houses examples of tropical plants, mammals, reptiles and exotic birds. Although it takes rather more of a pilgrimage to find the cultural centres in the city than it does the casinos, Southern Nevada's Allied Arts Council helps by supporting an active Cultural Focus Division aimed at promoting culture – to quote its modest claim – 'as another interesting dimension of the Las Vegas area'. This body ensures that the city's historical monuments, among several other desirable community assets, are properly preserved and promoted.

The Las Vegas Mormon Fort, at the corner of Las Vegas Boulevard North and Washington Avenue, has recently been taken over and refurbished by the city's own Preservation Association. This 150-foot long adobe-walled settlement was constructed in 1850 and might be classified as the very first wayside inn. Soon, saloons and gambling parlours opened to cater for the rough, tough miners and developers who had come to look over this rumbustious settlement in the desert.

Another sort of 'cultural' attraction is embodied in Liberace, the self-styled Mr. Showmanship. His brand of entertainment has been so popular in Las Vegas that his brother George is running a museum on East Tropicana Avenue devoted exclusively to his personality and his flamboyant style of dressing. Inside, past the piano-shaped reception desk, is a treasure-trove of exotic clothes, cars, pianos and extravagant bric-a-brac. Among the star exhibits is a red, white and blue Rolls Royce and a London taxi.

▶ *The Liberace Museum, in which the props and clothes which have made the entertainer a legend are on public display*

▼ *The majestic landscape of the Red Rock Canyon, just outside Las Vegas – a complete contrast to the clamour of the city*

His collection of pianos includes one Chopin played, a concert grand which belonged to George Gershwin, and a comprehensive range of miniature pianos. Among his clothes are a Czar Nicholas uniform with 22-carat gold braiding, and a reproduction of a coronation robe worn by King George V, topped by $60,000 worth of rare chinchilla. The proceeds of the museum go to the Liberace Foundation for the Performing and Creative Arts which gives financial support to young musicians.

As a Las Vegas resident, Liberace appears in a show from time to time at one of the major hotels. Over the years Las Vegas has lured several important personalities to live there. Its most controversial inhabitant was Howard Hughes, who ran his multi-million dollar empire of airline and film interests from the seclusion of a hotel suite from which it is said he never emerged – at least for anyone to see.

In less eccentric times he revelled in a reclusive life on a ranch a few miles out of the city. The ranch, once owned by Vera Krupp, widow of the German arms manufacturer, has secret passages built between bedrooms. Something of an eccentric herself, she was once tied up by robbers who got away with millions of dollars worth of jewellery, including the Krupp Diamond, the exquisite million-dollar stone which, after it was recovered, was bought by Richard Burton for his then wife, Elizabeth Taylor.

Kyle Ranch, in Carey Avenue at Crown Drive, epitomises even more so the strange alchemy which makes Las Vegas so potent. Numerous celebrated couples, many of them film stars and other showbiz personalities whose much-publicised marriages had failed, went there in the 1940s and 1950s to acquire the essential legal residential qualifications for a divorce.

Like the whole of Nevada, Las Vegas's history is in the timeless permanence of its scenery. Less than 20 miles west of the city is a typical example of nature's overwhelming superiority. Red Rock Canyon has an escarpment 3,000 foot high, sculptured in the most intricate variations of pinnacles and towers, and suffused in a rosy glow of rocks that makes the entire landscape look as if it is blushing.

This breathtaking high desert panorama can now be viewed on a 60-mile scenic drive.

Yet even with unlimited space to grow in all directions, Las Vegas gives the impression of being a very crowded place. At night the pavements on the Strip are packed, and the roads are choked. Although Nellis, one of the largest air training bases in the US Air Force, is only eight miles away, the military presence of 8,000 airmen and other personnel, is seldom noticeable among the crowds. Uniforms are rarely seen although the base has unobtrusively taken over the desert where the last outskirts of the city end.

The fact that Las Vegas has even come to terms with the brooding proximity of the Nuclear Test Site which begins its millions of acres of forbidden desert terrain 60 miles to the north-east of the city, shows that, like the pioneers who started it all nearly 150 years ago, Las Vegas has not lost the instinct for survival.

Nothing in the foreseeable future can stop this incongruous desert outpost from continuing to offer that elusive pot of gold at the end of the rainbow.

Las Vegas Directory

HOTELS

The hotels listed here are either recommended by the American Automobile Association (AAA) or have been selected because of their particular appeal to tourists. As a rough guide to cost, they have been classified as either expensive, moderate or inexpensive. All have bathrooms and colour television.

BARBARY COAST HOTEL: 3595 Las Vegas Blvd South, tel 737 7111. 160 rooms. Interior in the style of the 1890s. Casino. Restaurant. 24-hour coffeeshop. Moderate.

BEST WESTERN MARDI GRAS INN: 3500 Paradise Rd, tel 731 2020. 320 rooms. Colour TV. Pool. Slot-machine arcade. Queen-size beds. Moderate.

CAESARS PALACE: 3570 Las Vegas Blvd, tel 731 7110. 1227 rooms. Distinctive building in landscaped surroundings. Pool. Health club. Tennis. Casino and other entertainment. Expensive.

CIRCUS CIRCUS HOTEL: 2880 Las Vegas Blvd South, tel 734 0410. 800 rooms. Health club and sauna. Non-stop circus entertainment. Parking lot. Inexpensive.

EL MOROCCO HOTEL: 2975 Las Vegas Blvd South, tel 735 7145. 252 rooms. Arcade casino. Coffee-shop. Moderate.

FERGUSONS MOTEL DOWNTOWN: 1028 E Fremont St, tel 382 3500. 66 rooms. Heated pool. Family suites. Baby-sitting. Moderate.

FRONTIER HOTEL: 3120 Las Vegas Blvd South, tel 734 0110. 589 rooms. Suites. Valet parking. Putting green. Tennis. Four restaurants. Moderate.

HOLIDAY INN-DOWNTOWN: 300 N Main St, tel 385 1500. 418 rooms. Pool. Casino. 24-hour restaurant. Entertainment. Moderate.

THE INN AT LAS VEGAS: 1501 W Sahara Av, tel 732 3222. 239 rooms. Pool. Suites. Special non-smoker area. Moderate.

LAS VEGAS HILTON: 3000 Paradise Rd, tel 732 5111. 2,783 rooms. Conference centre. Pool. Putting. Tennis. Youth hostel. Restaurant. Top name entertainment. Expensive.

MGM GRAND HOTEL: 3645 Las Vegas Blvd South, tel 739 4111. 2108 rooms. The MGM is a tourist attraction in its own right, a completely self-contained resort you need never leave. Casino. Pool. Ten tennis courts. Health club. Restaurant. Entertainment. Expensive.

MOTEL MONACO: 3073 Las Vegas Blvd South, tel 735 9222. 70 rooms. Pool. Deposit required. Inexpensive.

RAINBOW VEGAS HOTEL: 401 S Casino Center Blvd, tel 386 6166. 280 rooms. Coin laundry. Pool. Inexpensive.

RIVIERA HOTEL: 2901 Las Vegas Blvd South, tel 734 5110. 1,209 rooms. Casino. Pool. Tennis. Health club. Restaurants. Entertainment. Expensive.

RODEWAY INN: 3786 Las Vegas Blvd South, tel 736 1434. 97 rooms. Large parking area. Heated pool. Inexpensive.

SAFARI MOTEL: 2001 E Fremont St, tel 384 4021. 23 rooms. Pool. Shower-baths. Inexpensive.

SAM'S TOWN HOTEL: 5111 Boulder Hwy, tel 456 7777. 200 rooms. Wild West décor. Pool. Casino. Restaurant and coffee-shop. Inexpensive.

SANDS HOTEL: 3355 Las Vegas Blvd South, tel 733 5000. 759 rooms. Set in landscaped grounds. Very good accommodation. Putting green. Two pools. Casino. Tennis. Health club. Moderate.

SKY RANCH MOTEL: 2009 E Fremont St, tel 382 2846. 29 rooms. Some two-roomed units. Pool. Inexpensive.

SOMERSET HOUSE MOTEL: 294 Convention Center Dr, tel 735 4411. 104 rooms. Pool. Coin laundry. Adjacent coffee-shop. Inexpensive.

UNION PLAZA HOTEL: 1 Main St, tel 386 2110. 504 rooms. Centrally-placed hotel. Pool. Parking lot. Casino. Restaurant and coffee-shop. Moderate.

RESTAURANTS

The restaurants listed below have been chosen either because they are recommended by the American Automobile Association (AAA) or for their appeal to tourists. They have been classified as either expensive, moderate, or inexpensive as a rough guide to cost.

ALPINE VILLAGE INN: 3003 Paradise Rd, tel 734 6888. The restaurant has a European atmosphere and specialises in Swiss and German food. Featured dishes include roast caponette, kohlrouladen, wienerschnitzel and German potato pancakes. Wide choice of beers. Children's menu. Moderate.

THE BACCHANAL: Caesars Palace, 3570 Las Vegas Blvd South, tel 731 7110. Setting resembles an ancient Roman garden. The lavish restaurant is named after Bacchus, the Roman god of wine. Expensive.

BENIHANA VILLAGE: Las Vegas Hilton, 3000 Paradise Rd, tel 732 5111. Delightfully set in a recreated Japanese village with running streams and oriental gardens. Hibachi-style cooking and special steaks. Expensive.

CARSON CITY RESTAURANT: Circus Circus Hotel, 2880 Las Vegas Blvd South, tel 734 0410. Excellent for family dining. Ringside seats available to watch the circus. Western-style food. Inexpensive.

DA VINCI'S: Maxim Hotel, 160 E Flamingo Rd, tel 731 4300. The restaurant is situated on the Strip's 'Golden Corner' and good food plus excellent service are the order of the day here. House special is Chicken da Vinci. Inexpensive.

DELMONICO ROOM: Riviera Hotel, The Strip, tel 734 5110. Elegant restaurant with a French-influenced menu. Inexpensive.

GREAT WALL: Sahara Sq. Elegant interior where you can sample superb Chinese food. Moderate.

LILIIE LANGTRY'S: Golden Nugget, 129 E Fremont St, tel 385 7111. Named after 'The Jersey Lily', actress and confidante of King Edward VII. Period décor and, oddly, a Cantonese menu. Moderate.

PHILLIPS SUPPER HOUSE: 4545 W Sahara Av, tel 873 5222. Pleasant restaurant featuring lobster and clambake, New England style. Moderate.

QUARTERDECK RESTAURANT: Mint Hotel, 100 E Fremont St, tel 385 7440. All aboard for this elegant restaurant with a strong maritime theme. Champagne buffets on Sunday evenings are very popular. Moderate.

TRANSPORT

AIRPORT: Las Vegas is served by McCarran International Airport which is five miles south of the business district via Paradise Road and The Strip. Like LA's LAX airport, McCarran is being generally modernised and updated. Over 800 million dollars are being invested over the next twenty years. It is predicted that the eventual passenger turnover per year will be in the region of 30 million. Currently 230 flights a day leave the airport, run by 15 major airlines.

CAR HIRE: There are many car hire firms operating in and around Las Vegas. A full list of addresses and telephones can be found in the local directory's Yellow Pages. Another source is *Vegas Visitor*, a newspaper for tourists. Favourite places for hire operators' offices are McCarran International Airport and The Strip. Members of the AAA may qualify for discounts from . Hertz and Avis on certain selected routes. Major operators are: Avis-Airport, tel 739 5595; Strip, tel 736 1935; Budget, tel 735 9311; National-Airport, tel 739 5391; Strip, tel 734 2222; Hertz-Airport, tel 736 4900; Strip, tel 735 4597.

TAXIS: Taxis are freely available at the entrance of major hotels, airports, casinos, central restaurants and cab-stands. The charge is determined by both the number of passengers and the distance to be travelled. There is a flat rate for the first fifth of a mile, with relatively lower rates for subsequent fifths of a mile. Cab-drivers expect around 15% of the fare as a tip. Long-distance travel by taxi can obviously work out rather expensive. Major companies are: ABC Union and Ace Cab Companies, tel 736 8383; Checker and Vegas Western Cab Companies, tel 736 6121; Desert and Western Cab Companies, tel 384 1672; Whittlesea Blue Cab, tel 384 6111; Yellow Cab, tel 382 4444.

BUSES: The downtown area is served by the Las Vegas Transit System. Buses run every quarter of an hour, 24 hours a day. The southern terminal is Hacienda Hotel at the end of The Strip. If frequent bus trips are envisaged, it would be wise to purchase a commuter ticket at a discount price. Otherwise, the exact fare will be required by the operator for one-off journeys. Useful bus service addresses are: Greyhound Lines, 220 S Main St; Trailways, 217 N 4th St.

TOURING INFORMATION

AAA CLUBS: Nevada is served by the California State Automobile Association. The Las Vegas HQ is at 3312 W Charleston Blvd, tel 870 9171.

LAS VEGAS CHAMBER OF COMMERCE: 2301 E Sahara Av, tel 457 4664.

LAS VEGAS CONVENTION AND VISITORS BUREAU: 3150 S Paradise Rd, tel 733 2323.

LAS VEGAS-TONOPAH-RENO STAGELINES AND TRANSPORT UNLIMITED: Both companies run bus tours around Las Vegas nightclubs, to the Hoover Dam, Grand Canyon and Death Valley. See Yellow Pages for address and telephone details.

MUSEUMS AND GALLERIES

ADOBE GALLERIES: 3110 Las Vegas Blvd, tel 733 2941. The six-gallery complex exhibits abstract paintings, items of Indian craft and a wealth of general interest art.

LIBERACE MUSEUM: 2½ miles E of The Strip, 1775 E Tropicana Av, tel 731 1775. An Aladdin's Cave of exotic clothes, cars and pianos. One of the many remarkable exhibits is an imperial Russian uniform with 22-carat-gold braiding.

SHOPPING

LAS VEGAS PLAZA: 3025 Las Vegas Blvd South. The Plaza is situated at the heart of The Strip and, in common with most other shops in this district, only closes on Sunday mornings. A special attraction of the Plaza is the shop of dress designer Suzy Creamcheese, a former go-go dancer known as 'Queen of the Hippies' back in the 1960s. Her talents have now turned in the direction of *haute couture* and she is now famed for her heavily-sequinned gear for the jet-set. Sammy Davis Jnr and Shirley Maclaine are among the famous names who have worn her creations. The clothes are displayed against a backcloth that depicts the Victorian era at its extravagant height.

THE BOULEVARD MALL AND SHOPPING CENTRE: 3528 Maryland Pkwy, tel 735 8268. This is a shopping centre that literally has everything. Centrally situated, a few minutes from The Strip, the complex boasts many attractions. There is an enormous car park with space for nearly 6,000 vehicles. Around 70 specialist outlets ranging from pet shops to trendy boutiques, plus four large department stores selling every conceivable article that a shopper could require. The centre is fully air-conditioned and trades seven days a week.

THE MEADOWS: 4300 Meadows Lane. Even larger than the Boulevard Mall Centre, this multi-million dollar addition to Las Vegas' shopping facilities is ultra-modern in design. As well as hundreds of interesting shops the centre contains several coffee-shops and restaurants.

SPORT

GOLF: Las Vegas has plenty of fine golf courses for the touring enthusiast. Below are just some of the local courses (which may be attached to hotels). Craig Ranch GC, Desert Inn GC, Dunes Hotel GC, Sahara-Nevada Hotel GC, Tropicana Hotel GC, Winterwood GC.

LAS VEGAS SPORTING HOUSE: 3025 Industrial Rd, tel 733 8999. A superlative health farm offering the best range of sporting facilities in Las Vegas by far. Apart from a 60-foot-long swimming-pool and a fully-equipped gymnasium, the centre boasts saunas, steam rooms, jacuzzi baths, massage parlours, tennis and squash courts and even beauty parlours and hairdressing salons. The chance of spotting one of the many famous names who frequent the centre should add to your enjoyment.

RODEOS: If you plan on visiting Las Vegas in May, 'Helldorado' is *the* western event that should not be missed. For further details, tel 733 2323.

THE ROLLER PALACE: 800 E Karen Av, tel 732 1046. The American obsession for high-speed roller-skating is amply catered for here. Just hire some skates and rumble round the stadium. Sometimes a live band plays background music. Stadium opens evenings only.

SHOWBOAT HOTEL: 2800 E Fremont St, tel 385 9123. An opportunity to take the family bowling at what must be the largest and best-equipped bowling alley in the world. The Showboat has no less than 106 lanes. Also in the building is a snack bar and a free crèche for the younger children.

PLACES OF INTEREST

BINION'S HORSESHOE: 128 Fremont St. The main feature of this casino is a huge golden horseshoe. Suspended from the lucky emblem are sections of bullet-proof glass which protect 100 American banknotes. The notes are unique in that they each display the head of Salmon Portland Chase. This well-known statesman was secretary of the treasury from 1861–1864, the period of the American Civil War. He built his reputation by successfully defending runaway slaves from the Deep South. In 1864 he was appointed Chief Justice and, as such, presided over the impeachment of Andrew Jackson. Each note bearing his image is worth $10,000.

CIRCUS CIRCUS: The Strip, tel 734 0410. Situated in the hotel of the same name, the establishment combines the excitement of the circus with the extravagance of the casino. The gambling area has been built as a circus tent and boldly painted in pink-and-white stripes. The 'Big Top' is open from 11.30 am to midnight and among the many featured acts are trapeze stars, clowns, unicyclists and illusionists. There is a viewing gallery where children may watch from above, but they are obviously not allowed on the casino floor.

MINT HOTEL AND CASINO: First and Fremont Sts, tel 385 7440. A special feature of this casino is that it allows the potential gambler to view the gaming house from behind the scenes. A one-way mirror gives visitors the opportunity to look down on the gaming tables in secret. Another attraction is an exposed version of an old-style slot machine displaying all the internal mechanism.

OLD NEVADA: 17 miles W on Blue Diamond Rd. An old town restored in the style of a western frontier community. Its features include shootouts, lynchings and ragtime piano-playing.

OLD VEGAS: 2440 Boulder Hwy, Henderson, tel 564 1311. The site, some 15 miles west of Las Vegas, was originally occupied by a Mormon adobe fort, but has been converted into a theme park depicting the early history of a Nevada settlement. Among the many items of interest to visitors are a railway museum, a narrow-gauge steam-train, a Wild West shooting gallery and an old fairground roundabout. An entirely reconstructed street contains frontier shops and stores selling a variety of souvenirs.

RED ROCK CANYON AREA: on W Charleston Blvd, 16 miles W of Las Vegas. A desert beauty spot with breathtaking scenery. The steep and angular red and white sandstone canyons offer a starkly different visual experience from the bright lights of Las Vegas.

VALLEY OF FIRE STATE PARK: 30 miles E of Las Vegas near Boulder Canyon. Scenic area formed by a six-mile-long natural basin. Interesting varieties of rock and sandstone erosion. The 46,000-acre park has many walking trails, a visitor centre and picnicking facilities.

WESTWORLD: Boulder Hwy, Henderson. An entertainment complex featuring pioneer and western characters, plus Elvis Presley movies.

CASINOS OF LAS VEGAS: Besides the casinos mentioned above, there are many others located along The Strip. They include Caesars Palace, Desert Inn, Hacienda, The Flamingo, The Riviera, The Sands, Las Vegas Hilton, MGM Grand Hotel, The Marina, The Maxim, Stardust, Landmark, The Frontier and The Tropicana. The main games played are craps, blackjack (sometimes called '21'), roulette, poker, keno and baccarat. Casinos in the downtown area of Las Vegas (Fremont St) also abound and include the world famous Golden Nugget.

THEATRES AND CINEMAS

DRIVE-IN MOVIES: A popular style of entertainment in Las Vegas. Two of the top ones are: The Sunset, 3800 Cheyenne Av, tel 648 7550 and The Nevada, 3873 Las Vegas Blvd N, tel 643 3333.

MEADOWS PLAYHOUSE: 4775 S Maryland Pkwy, tel 739 3131. The theatre has a permanently-based repertory company that features both modern and classical plays.

RED ROCK THEATERS: 5201 W Charleston Blvd, tel 870 1423. Eleven cinemas under one roof, each showing a different movie.

UNIVERSITY OF NEVADA: The Judy Bayley Theater seats 600 and specialises in ballet and dance revues. Also on the campus is the Artemus Ham Concert Hall, where leading virtuosi perform with distinguished visiting orchestras. Here the seating capacity is 2,000.

NIGHTLIFE

THE STRIP: The Mecca for entertainment and nightlife in Las Vegas is The Strip. A 5-mile-long wonderland of showbiz razzmatazz famed the world over. Multi-million dollar extravaganzas boast all the top names, emblazoned in lights.

DISCOS: Dozens of discothèques cater for the more energetic visitors. One of the top discos is Jubilation, 75 E Harmon Av, tel 733 8822. The Jubilation is an exotic piece of modern architecture owned by the entertainer Paul Anka. There is every chance of tripping the light fantastic alongside top celebrities at this lavish dance-hall.

CLIMATE

The summers in Las Vegas are hot and dry, and in June, July and August the midday temperatures are very high, but the humidity is low. Good air-conditioning helps dispel any discomfort indoors. Winters are usually mild, but the nights can be cold and it is often windy. This is the best season for outdoor activities.

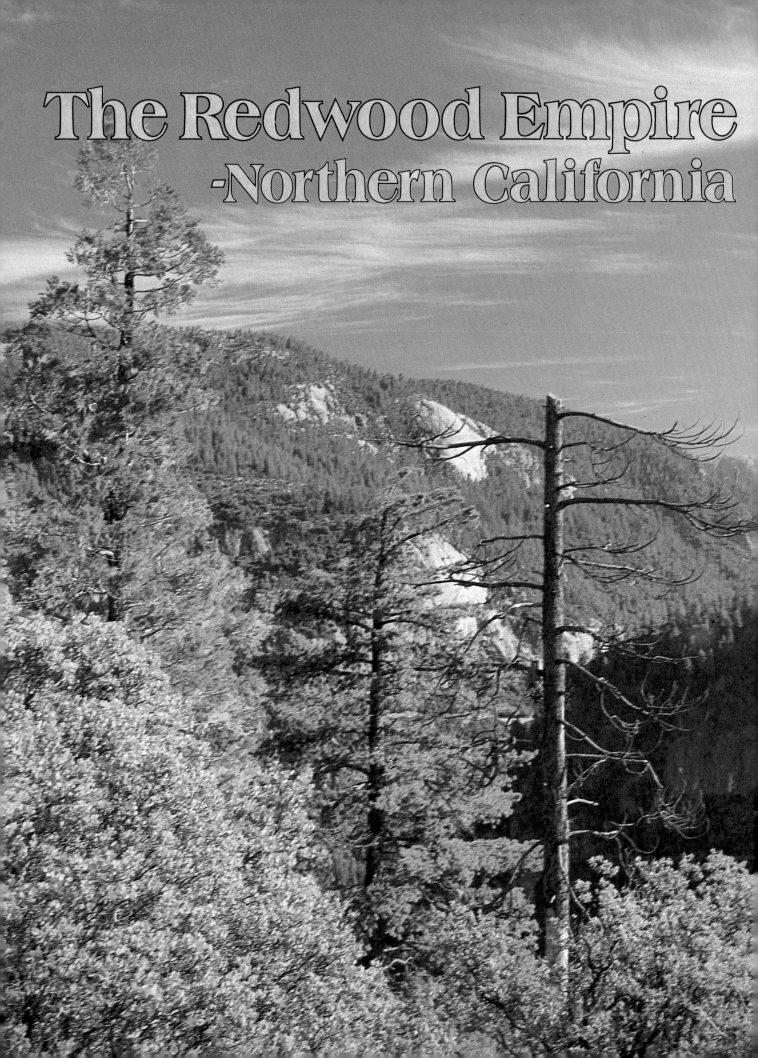

The Redwood Empire
-Northern California

Gold brought prosperity and people to northern California as it did to the southern half of the state. But the California which unveils itself beyond San Francisco is different to the one which holds glittering Los Angeles close to its heart.

Gone are the sun-baked deserts and glamorous resorts; this is a land of cool forests and warm valleys, their hillsides sheltering vineyards.

This is not an international playground, but more a national parkland, where the glossy limousines of the south give way to family campers and rough-clad hikers on foot.

It is a region in which to go out and explore, with many parts of differing character and personality. The coast is rugged and dramatic, offering wild seascapes and casual workaday fishing villages.

Inland, around the Napa and Sonoma valleys, is the centre of the state's wine country, fostering a calm Continental air, whereas north of San Francisco is a truly American phenomenon, the Redwood Empire, where the greatest trees in the world have their exclusive domain. Their provinces stretch northwards into the Russian River region, a wild and beautiful area of rugged grandeur, searched out by those looking for a taste of the outdoor life.

The high-life is not, however, found wanting. There is San Francisco, where elegant living is to be had, and there are the mountain resorts around Lake Tahoe which, divided by the California–Nevada state line, has on the Nevada side all the glamour of the gambling casinos and the 20th-century comforts that the state has to offer.

Yosemite National Park – a wilderness of high mountains and deep valleys, rushing rivers and tumbling waterfalls, groves of giant sequoias, pine, fir and oak, and alpine meadows bedecked with wild flowers

The differences between the southern and northern halves of California are as marked as the contrasts between each of its principal cities – Los Angeles and San Francisco. Both areas, however, enjoy uninterrupted and unrivalled views of the Pacific Ocean from apparently limitless expanses of soft, sandy beaches. North of San Francisco, the terrain acquires a gaunter outline, derived from row upon row of majestic mountain ranges, and the more rugged vegetation they support.

The Coastal Ranges stretch almost vertically from the Oregon boundary to Los Angeles – a maze of ridges and plains covered in a rich stubble of forests and shrubs. A part of these is grandly known as the Redwood Empire – thousands of square miles of majestic trees dominating much of the northern landscape. Cleaving through their serried ranks the Redwood Highway (US 101) stretches for 450 miles, from San Francisco's Golden Gate to the borders of Oregon. From time to time detours penetrate clusters of giant redwoods, and one stretch, 200 miles from San Francisco, turns into the old highway for 25 miles, free of fretting fast traffic, permitting the tourist to stop and admire some of the oldest and tallest trees on earth. Several of these 'Monarchs of the Forest', often referred to by their Latin names, *Sequoia Giganteum*

(giant redwoods) and *Sequoia Sempervirens* (coastal redwoods), are over 2,000 years old.

Another 100 miles to the north lies the 106,000-acre Redwood National Park, situated in the heart of northern California's lumber lands. But the timber industry does not have it all its own way these days, for the lofty redwood groves throughout these parts are well protected from the chainsaw. Many of these groves are financed by charitable organisations, or are kept as memorials – some to private individuals, and some to public figures. Without this patronage many of the ancient trees would have been felled by the lumber interests. The lead was taken in 1918 when three eminent conservationists formed the Save the Redwoods League. By 1921 they had raised enough money to buy the first grove beside the Eel River, which flows north from its source near the Mendocino National Forest and has its estuary a few miles south of Eureka. Here the first acreage was named after an American soldier who died in World War I. By the end of 1976, more than 450 redwood groves had been established in the state – notably one in memory to the former United Nations Secretary General, Dag Hammarskjöld, who died in a plane crash in September 1961. Another in Humboldt State Park, south of Eureka, touchingly remembers

The magnificent redwood, an evergreen coniferous tree native to the Pacific coast from Oregon south through California, is thought to be the tallest tree in the world

children who died in infancy.

In the early days a redwood grove could be bought for just a few hundred dollars. Now a single tree can cost $8,000 or more. It took John D Rockefeller Jnr, a member of the fabulously rich American family, to acquire the largest area of all – 27,000 acres of forest and fields named the Rockefeller Forest in part of the Humboldt Redwoods State Park. Situated on the Eel River, where it meets the Bull Creek, south of Eureka, the forest was a favourite picnic site for the Rockefeller family who, thanks to their interest, wrested it from the clutches of the Pacific Lumber Company in the 1920s. The forest starts about 50 miles north of Eureka, which has been an important lumber centre since the 1850s.

Eureka reflects the fortunes the lumber barons made from the virgin forests of northern California during the last century. Though the affluent era has now passed, the ornate Victorian houses where they lived still stand in pristine condition. The Carson Mansion, for instance, though closed to the public, is certainly worth taking the time to view at 2nd and M Streets.

EUREKA

Hotels

CARSON HOUSE INN: 1209 4th St, tel 443 1601. 45 rooms. Moderate-expensive.

MATADOR MOTEL: 129 4th St, tel 443 9751. 25 rooms. Moderate.

RED LION MOTOR INN: 1929 4th St, tel 445 0844. 179 rooms. Expensive.

Restaurants

LAZIO'S SEAFOOD RESTAURANT: 4 C St, on Humboldt Bay, tel 442 2337. Cocktails and lounge, also a take-away service. Moderate.

VOLPI'S RESTAURANT: 6269 Loma St, tel 442 1376. Italian and American cuisine with seafood the speciality. Children's menu. Moderate.

Places of interest

FORT HUMBOLDT: Exhibits chart early logging methods. Building was formerly the HQ of US Grant in 1853.

HUMBOLDT BAY HARBOUR CRUISE: leaves from C St, tel 443 2741. 1¼-hour afternoon bay trips.

diameter, frail forest flowers and rushing streams. The forest wildlife includes chipmunks, racoons and deer. There are also a café and shop where many unusual gifts fashioned out of redwood are available.

Muir Woods is one of many environmental benefits which John Muir fought for and won. Throughout most of his 76 years he worked obsessively to preserve America's natural resources and to establish national parks and forest reserves. Born in 1838 in Dunbar, Scotland, he was largely unrewarded for his work until, at the age of 42, he married Louise Strentzel, daughter of a Polish immigrant who became known as the 'Father of Californian Horticulture'. The marriage happily provided the basis for Muir's campaigning zeal. The couple went to live in Martinez, a suburb a few miles to the east. Louise's parents left them a ranch which Muir and Louise expanded, and later turned into a successful fruit farm. Muir's main preoccupation, however, was with conservation and natural history, and he wrote copiously on the urgent need to save America's natural heritage of trees and forests, both as watersheds and as places of solitude and wilderness. His persuasive

CRESCENT CITY

Hotels

BEST WESTERN CURLY REDWOOD LODGE: 701 Redwood Hwy, tel 464 2137. 36 rooms. Moderate.

CRESCENT TRAVELODGE: 725 Hwy 101 N, tel 464 6106. 52 rooms. Moderate.

PACIFIC MOTOR HOTEL: 1 mile N on US 101, tel 464 4141. 62 rooms. Moderate.

Restaurant

HARBOR VIEW GROTTO: ½ mile S, 1 blk W of US 101, Citizen's Dock Rd, tel 464 3815. Fishing-boat views. Varied menu features steak and seafood. Moderate.

Places of Interest

OLD LIGHTHOUSE: on Battery Pt, tel 464 3089. A museum features the original light, early clocks and nautical photographs.

UNDERSEA GARDENS: Anchor Way. Interesting collection of marine flora and fauna viewed from underwater windows. Regular scuba-diving displays.

Crescent City's Del Norte Coast Redwoods State Park, eight miles south of the city, on the Redwood Highway, has four memorial redwood groves, the steep slopes on which they stand reaching almost to the ocean. A National Tribute Grove, east of the city, which is California's most northern community of any size, is dedicated to the memory of the fallen of both world wars. Many of the magnificent trees in the grove were 'bought' by bereaved parents, and more than 5,000 people made donations.

Not that one needs to travel hundreds of miles out of San Francisco to be among these 'ambassadors from another time', as author John Steinbeck called the giant species of redwood. On the south-west slopes of Mount Tamalpais, about 20 miles from the city, is Muir Woods, a 550-acre redwood grove where some of the trees tower 240 feet high. The oldest has an estimated age of 1,200 years. Early this century the trees were to be felled to make way for a giant reservoir, but were saved by California's political reformer, William Kent, who had bought the land and all its trees (then called Redwood Canyon) for $45,000. He enlisted the support of President Theodore Roosevelt and persuaded him to declare the area a national monument in 1908. It was named Muir Woods after the renowned Scottish-born conservationist, John Muir. Visitors to the wood can inspect a cross-section of a fallen tree, which was alive before William the Conqueror invaded England in 1066, or follow six miles of forest trails which pass by massive trunks of more than 13 feet in

Seals are a common sight along the rugged northern Californian coast

arguments impressed President Theodore Roosevelt so much that during his presidency more than 148 million acres of national forest, 23 national monuments and five national parks were established for the nation's enjoyment.

The 17-room mansion where John Muir lived for 24 years – it is on a very steep hill for which special transport is available – is surrounded by orchards and vineyards. It can be seen as it was furnished at the turn of the century. Their first home, a Spanish-style abode, later used by Muir's daughter, can also be visited. The ranch-house was built in 1849 by Vicente Martinez after whom the town was also named.

Drive another hour and quarter north to another State Park, and you will come face to face with reminders that, even 200 years ago, there were signs of an early East–West conflict. This emerged particularly at Fort Ross, one of the oldest, though lesser known landmarks. In determined sorties across the world in search of expansion and trade, a Russian expedition in 1812 landed on a rocky bay on the west coast. They built a stockaded fort and called it Rossiya, Russian for Russia. The word was later shortened to Ross. Joined by Indians, 700

Muscovites harvested seal and otter pelts and in one year alone shipped more than 3,500 of these skins back to Sitka in Alaska, where the Tsarists had established their first North Pacific base.

Although the Spaniards had already laid nominal claim to this stretch of the coast, the Russians maintained a firm foothold on the American mainland and in 1821 tried to impose further authority. An imperial decree from Tsar Alexander I closed the Pacific coast north of San Francisco to all except Russian ships. Two years later, the United States President, James Monroe, issued his famous doctrine, triggered off by European intervention in South America, which warned that the American Continents 'are henceforth not to be considered as subjects for future colonization by any European powers'.

When Alaska was sold to the United States (it cost her just a few cents per acre) in 1867, the menacing 'Russian Bear' sensibly withdrew to the frozen wastes of Siberia, but reminders of the Russian presence persist in northern California. For instance, the Russian River was originally named Slavianka by the Russian colonists. From its source in the Coast Ranges near

Ukiah, north of Redwood Valley, it flows south until it turns sharply west to empty into the Pacific near Jenner, a few miles south of Fort Ross.

As the notorious San Andreas Fault runs along the coast near Fort Ross, the 1906 San Francisco earthquake left little of the chapel and only part of the stockade built by the Russians. Later this century the Federal State Park system acquired the fort, and on 19 June 1974 the park was opened to the public with the chapel, the commandant's house, the seven- and eight-sided block houses and stockade meticulously rebuilt with hand-sawn Redwood timbers. The restoration was based on old plans uncovered in Moscow archives. Though Fort Ross is open every day, it is especially highlighted four times a year when events are held to commemorate its colourful history. On Memorial Day (the last Monday in May), and Independence Day (4th July), there are Russian Orthodox Church ceremonies, and in late summer and mid-autumn, the Indians hold food festivals and tribal dances, and display Indian crafts.

The cold, calm waters of Lake Helen, in the Lassen Volcanic National Park

The Russian River in the 1930s, when the area first became popular with tourists

Like southern California, the northern part of the state was also 'colonised' from the east by prospectors, who were urged on by promises of fortunes and a golden future to 'Go West Young Man'. Throughout the second half of the 19th-century, thousands of Americans did just that. They imposed an even greater domination on parts of the state than was ever exerted by the Russians, the indigenous Indians (who lost much of their territorial inheritance), the Spanish and Mexican adventurers or the British privateers such as Sir Francis Drake.

Many of the settlers in the northern half of the state would have needed to cross the Shasta-Trinity National Forest, part of which is in the approaches to the Cascade mountain range and part in the Coast Ranges area. Situated between, and about 100 miles from the coast, is the curiously named 100,000-acre Whiskeytown-Shasta-Trinity National Recreation Area. This nature reserve has four major dam-created lakes and many recreational and camping facilities.

Beside the Clair Engle Lake, Trinity Center is a small town of 2,300 people distinguished by its museum collection of barbed wire. Nearly 500 samples of 700 known basic patents are on display – thanks to the interest shown in this vital outdoor commodity by Edwin Scott, pioneer of Trinity County, whose lifetime collection this was. He opened the museum named after him in 1962. Trinity Center was once the main route linking Oregon and California, and his museum, reflecting the importance of the former staging post, in-cludes a display of essential household items of the 19th century, like smoothing irons (some of the two dozen shown are heated with charcoal, some with gasolene and some even with electricity), hand-operated washing machines, a pack saddle for oxen, horses and mules, and snow shoes for horses. It also houses a stagecoach and other early vehicles.

Further east is the 106,000-acre Lassen Volcanic National Park, surrounded by 1.2 million acres of national forest where the Cascades join the Sierra Nevada. The park is dominated by Lassen Peak, a 10,457-foot high dormant volcano which unexpectedly blew its top in 1914, and continued to growl for seven years afterwards. Even now a small halo of steam can be seen now and again crowning the summit. Three other volcanoes still exist – Cinder Cone (6,907 feet), Prospect Peak (8,338 feet), and Mount Harkness (8,045 feet) – the summits of each are accessible along marked trails. There are also many lava flows, hot springs, boiling lakes and mudpots in the park, the latter emitting highly sulphuric odours from ominously gurgling pools of hot mud.

Near the Oregon boundary, the Lava Beds National Monument is another re-minder of the turbulent soil on which California rests. Centuries ago, flaming volcanoes fashioned the rocks in this craggy terrain. Lava formed deep chasms, and nearly 300 caverns were created on what became a 46,500-acre expanse of cinder cones. During the only Indian war fought by the United States inside California, these caves formed natural protection for the Indian warriors.

The most accessible demonstration of the earth's mighty power is to be found within two hour's drive of San Francisco in the north-east corner of the state near Geyser-ville. The town is about 80 miles north of the city on US 101 in the heart of geyser country. Though there are no true geysers in Geyserville, it claims to be in the largest geothermal area in the world. For a specta-cular performance, you will need to drive a few miles south-east to Calistoga, the home of Old Faithful. This is the name given to

---

LASSEN VOLCANIC NATIONAL PARK

Hotel

DRAKESBAD GUEST RANCH: 47 miles SE of Park Headquarters; 17 miles NW of Chester on CR Chester–Warner Valley, tel Susanville operator, Drakesbad number 2. 17 rooms. Expensive.

Places of Interest

BUMPASS HELL TRAIL: $\frac{1}{2}$ mile beyond Emerald Lake, leads off the Lassen Park Rd. large area of spectacular hot springs, boiling pools and mud pots.

CINDER CONE: accessible by trail from Butte and Summit Lakes. Fantastic lava beds and multi-coloured volcanic debris. Some of the flows occurred as recently as 1850–51.

SUMMIT LAKE: 5 miles NE of Kings Creek Meadows on the Park Rd. Lakeside camping grounds, hiking and fishing centre of the park.

one of the largest geysers in the world, for only two others merit this pet name – one in Yellowstone Park, Wyoming, and the other in North Island, New Zealand.

Surrounded by thick bamboo and plumed pampas grass, Old Faithful spits out a 60-foot high jet of hot steam and water every 40 minutes or so. The exact frequency depends on barometric pressure, moon, tides and other geological factors. In the process it ejects thousands of gallons of water which, as the fountain catches the sunlight, produces a breath-taking, rainbow-hued curtain of falling water. With so much thermal activity in the area, Calistoga has become a health spa. Old Faithful, situated on Tubbs Lane on the north side of Calistoga, is open between 9am and dusk every day, winter and summer.

California's rich earth also yields the fine grapes which produce its best-known wines. The Napa Valley on US 101 north of San Francisco is flanked by vineyards of all kinds and sizes. What the Americans call wineries cater enthusiastically for visitors.

Nearby, in a valley running almost parallel, is Sonoma, which can become part of a day's circular motoring tour. Sebastiani, 389 4th St E, one of California's oldest

78

family concerns, and Buena Vista Winery, 18000 Old Winery Rd, founded in 1857 by a Hungarian and once the largest winery in the world, are both prescribed stopping places in the Sonoma Valley. In Napa, look out for the Christian Brothers' Mont La Salle Vineyards, at 4411 Redwood Road.

Vineyards flourish on the warm slopes of the narrow Napa Valley, the heart of California's wine-growing region

Run for almost 100 years to support novitiates, its four impressive cellars receive more tourists than any other winery in the Napa Valley.

Further north, Domaine Candon at Yountville, off California Drive, produces champagne, the Chandon Napa Valley Brut

THE WINCHESTER MYSTERY HOUSE

This strangest of houses has attached to it an equally strange history. Sarah L Winchester left Newhaven, Connecticut, where she had married the heir to the Winchester arms fortune, after her husband had died of tuberculosis, and her six-week old daughter had contracted a rare and fatal disease. A spiritualist convinced her that the lives of her husband and daughter had been taken by the spirits of those killed with Winchester rifles, and that she also would die unless she began to build a mansion which would never be finished.

With a daily income of $1,000 and backed by a fortune of 20 million dollars, she took an eight-room house on what is now 525 South Winchester Boulevard, San José, and began her task. Foundations were laid in 1884. By the time of her death in 1922 (she was 83 years old), the house had cost 5½ million dollars.

It contains 160 rooms, 10,000 windows, 2,000 doors, 47 fireplaces, 40 bedrooms, 6 kitchens, 40 stairways and 52 skylights. The figure 13 is prominent throughout the rambling wooden mansion; 13 bathrooms, 13 hangers in a closet, chandeliers have 13 lights and one room has 13 windows.

The interior is beautifully furnished, with exquisite chandeliers of gold and silver, inlaid doors, stained-glass windows, parquet floors and wood panelling. The treasures contained within seem endless, and come from all over the world.

The house is also littered with devices for foiling the evil spirits which beleaguered her; some stairs lead nowhere, go up and down with steps only two inches high; corridors end at a fake door; doors open into space or on to blank walls. Even her servants needed a map to find their way around.

There are guided tours of both the house and grounds.

and the Chandon Blanc de Noirs being the best-known of the French-style champagnes. Further north again, Hanns Kornell Champagne Cellars, 1091 Larkmead Lane, St Helena, has only been in operation since 1958, but is already one of the few Californian wineries specialising in the traditional *champenoise* method of production, while Robert Mondavi Winery, 7801 St Helena Highway, Oakville; Inglenook 1991 St Helena Highway, Rutherford; and Louis Martini Winery, 254 St Helena Highway, are other notable vineyards in the area.

California's wine-growing regions extend as far south as Escondido, near San Diego in southern California. A vineyard in Saratoga, about 40 miles south of San Francisco, is notable for summer weekend concerts, as well as being the place where some of California's most famous wines are bottled and shipped all over the world. The Paul Masson vineyard, 13150 Saratoga Avenue, shows off its champagne and wine cellars by taking guests on an electronically guided tour, and presents the history of the company through an audio-visual show.

About 15 miles to the east is another great wine-growing centre. The oldest city in California, (it was founded in 1777), San José is renowned for its output of table wines. With more than half a million people, its population is only 100,000 below that of San Francisco, and boasts a big-city array of attractions. It has a planetarium attached to the Rosicrucian Egyptian Museum, and an observatory on the summit of Mount Hamilton, about 19 miles from the city at the end of a narrow winding road, 4,200 feet up. Its most unusual tourist draw is the Winchester Mystery House, built by Sarah L Winchester, widowed daughter-in-law of the inventor and manufacturer of the Winchester Repeater rifle (see box).

About 60 miles north-east of San Francisco, Sacramento embodies the gold-rush fever of 130 years ago. Fittingly, it is the

capital of California, with a population of 262,000. Here, in 1839, Captain John A Sutter laid the foundations of the adobe house that was to become Sutter's Fort – the first outpost of the white man in the Californian interior. The house has been restored and shows relics of the pioneering days. The State Capitol, built between 1861

This shining white dome belongs to the State Capitol in Sacramento, a building noted for its fine architecture

Emerald Bay, Lake Tahoe; clear blue water, pine-clad slopes and 4,000-foot-high mountains on the California-Nevada border

STOCKTON

Hotels

EDEN PARK INN: 1005 N Eldorado St, tel 466 2711. 60 rooms. Moderate.

BEST WESTERN CHARTER WAY INN: 550 W Charter Way, tel 948 0321. 82 rooms. Moderate.

VAGABOND MOTOR HOTEL: 33 N Center St, tel 948 6151. 102 rooms. Moderate.

Restaurants

ON LOCK SAM: 333 Sutter St, tel 466 4561. Cantonese Cuisine. Cocktails and lounge. Inexpensive-moderate.

YE OLDE HOOSIER INN: 1537 N Wilson Way. A family restaurant decorated with rare and beautiful antiques. Children's menu. Inexpensive.

Places of Interest

PIONEER MUSEUM AND HAGGEIN GALLERIES: at Rose St and Pershing Av in Victory Park. European and American paintings and objets d'art. Local historical items also displayed.

PIXIE WOODS WONDERLAND: in Louis Park. Children's play park with theme features based on fairy-tales and legends. Afternoon theatre.

and 1874, opens its doors daily to tourists who can admire the lofty dome 237 feet up, the murals and art exhibits inside, or enjoy the trees, shrubs and plants from all parts of the world in the surrounding park.

Like Sacramento, Stockton, a town 40 miles to the south, is linked by the Deepwater Ship Channel to San Francisco Bay. The town is the site of the University of the Pacific – the first chartered university in California. Many smaller Californian places have familiar names because of their association with gold. Placerville, for instance, about 20 miles east of Sacramento, made the wild West headlines because of a

famous robbery, which took place about 14 miles east of the town. On 30 June 1864, six men held up two coaches of the Pioneer Stageline from Virginia City. They took eight sacks of bullion and Wells Fargo treasure, brazenly gave a receipt purported to come from the Confederate States of America, and made off into the dust. All of them were eventually captured or killed. Known as the Bullion Bend Robbery, the incident is commemorated by a stone monument at the spot. Later the town earned its nickname of Hangtown, having adopted the expedient habit of hanging its law-breakers in pairs.

All along the foothills of the Sierra Nevada, souvenirs of rough, tough settlements remain. Mariposa, situated in what the pioneers called Mother Lode country, has the oldest courthouse still in use in California, built in 1854. Angels Camp is where Mark Twain found much of his material for his famous short story, *The Celebrated Jumping Frog of Calaveras County*, and there is a Jumping Frog Jubilee every May to recall the work. Another lawless town was Bodie, near the Nevada boundary on the eastern side of the Sierra Nevada. Here, in its heyday, 10,000 miners dug almost 100 million dollars worth of ore from the ground, and in the process made the town the most notorious gold mining camp in the west. Several of its buildings are maintained in a state of arrested disintegration – that means they will not be restored, but they will not be allowed to disintegrate further.

Life was certainly cheap in those days. To cross the plains from the east was a feat of endurance. The 1,400 people who now live in Truckee, just inside the Cali-

fornia–Nevada boundary, are proud of the Donner Memorial State Park of 350 acres which commemorates one of the greatest epic journeys undertaken in California. It is named after the organiser of a party of 89 pioneers who set out in April 1846 from Springfield, Illinois, in a wagon-train to cross to the west coast. Only 47 survived, having staggered on day after day through appalling terrain and endured terrible hardship. Those who died became food for those who lived.

Just south is the two-thirds portion of Lake Tahoe which lies inside California. Because it cannot offer the liberal gambling and marital arrangements mainly enjoyed by the other third, which is in Nevada, the many attractions consist of outdoor sporting and recreational facilities.

In a state with so much natural beauty, so many extremes and superlatives, where can be found the world's largest life-form (giant redwoods), the tallest known life-form (coastal redwoods), and the oldest known life-form (bristlecone pines), it is hard to select the one beauty spot which outshines all the others. However, the Yosemite National Park (see page 85) comes close to it; 1,200 square miles of magnificent mountains, valleys, forest and rivers, with at its heart the splendour of Yosemite Valley, the jewel at the centre of northern California's crown.

LAKE TAHOE

Hotels

BEST WESTERN STATION HOUSE INN: 901 Park Av, tel 542 1101. 100 rooms. Expensive.

CEDAR LODGE: corner of Cedar and Friday Avs, tel 544 6453. 32 rooms. Expensive.

SOUTH TAHOE TRAVELODGE: 1½ miles W of Casino center on US 50, tel 544 5266. 59 rooms. Expensive.

THE VIKING MOTOR LODGE: Cedar Av, tel 541 5155. 58 rooms. Moderate.

Restaurants

THE CHART HOUSE: 1½ miles off US 50, on Kingsbury Grade, tel 588 6276. Marvellous view of the lake from the dining room, which features steak and seafood. Children's menu. Moderate-expensive.

THE FOREST RESTAURANT: 18th floor of Harrah's Tahoe Hotel. Forest décor, beautifully furnished, with buffet. Children's menu. Moderate.

Places of Interest

PONDEROSA RANCH: on SR 28 in Incline Village, tel 831 0691. Re-creation of the set of TV's Bonanza series. General store, museum, evening barbecues and horseback riding.

VIKINGSHOLM: SW end of Emerald Bay. Clever reproduction of a 9th-century Norse fortress. Accessible by boat or steep 1-mile hike.

The vast complex of Stanford University, outside Palo Alto

San José and Monterey Bay

3 days – 265 miles

San Francisco – Redwood City – Palo Alto – Santa Clara – Saratoga – Los Gatos – San José – San Juan Bautista – Big Basins Redwood State Park – Santa Cruz – San Francisco

Drive south on US 101 for 20 miles to Redwood City.

Redwood City

The famous attraction here is a 65-acre complex combining zoo and oceanarium some four miles northeast of the city. Marine World/Africa USA has many wild animals roaming freely behind natural barriers formed by waterways. As well as dolphins, killer whales and seals, lions, elephants and chimpanzees perform in live shows. A 'jungle raft' safari is an exciting experience for all the family, while the camel and elephant rides are popular among children. Other amenities include a free, supervised playground, and refreshments.

Continue south on US 101 for 6 miles to Palo Alto.

Palo Alto

Stanford University, standing in an 8,200-acre estate known as 'Stanford Farm', dominates the city. Leland Stanford, the 19th-century railway magnate and senator, founded the university in 1891. Sited about a mile from the city centre, the observation platform of the Hoover Tower offers a panoramic view of the campus. The tower itself houses the Hoover Institution of War, Revolution and Peace, which is devoted to the study of world conflict. President Herbert Hoover, elected to the White House in 1928, is the famous graduate commemorated by the tower.

Worth visiting are the Stanford Art Gallery and the Leland Stanford Jnr Museum, which displays a collection of Egyptian antiques, oriental art, Rodin bronzes and mementoes of the Stanford family, including the original 'golden spike' which Leland Stanford hammered into the last sleeper to complete America's first transcontinental railway in 1869.

Buskers playing at Santa Clara County Fair

For the scientifically-minded, the two-mile-long linear electron accelerator which explores the particles of the atom is a unique attraction. The largest scientific instrument in the world, it cost over 100 million dollars to build.

Continue south on US 101 for 10 miles to Santa Clara.

Santa Clara

Prepare yourself for a rollicking experience as you approach Santa Clara, for Marriott's Great America, at the junction of Great America Parkway and US 101, awaits you. This 200-acre entertainment park evokes America's past through skilful landscaping and architecture. Several areas represent a specific theme such as the famous French Quarter of New Orleans or an 1890s Gold Rush town in the Klondike. It has shops, restaurants and incredible amusements.

No fewer than 30 thriller rides include the 'Willard's Whizzer', a roller coaster which spins riders into 70-degree banked turns; the Tidal Wave, a looping roller coaster which catapults riders backwards and forwards through a 75-foot-high vertical loop at 50 miles an hour, and the Logger's Run and Yankee Clipper Flume Rides, which propel those who dare on a winding, watery journey climaxing in a 60-foot plunge into a lagoon! Younger children can enjoy a narrow gauge railway, a zoo, dodgems and Fort Fun – an adventure area with tunnels, pools and slides. Bugs bunny and other cartoon characters are likely to be strolling around.

An array of restaurants offers every conceivable type of cuisine and you can round off the day by a visit to the park theatre or

Lockheed's Pictorium, which has the largest motion picture screen in the world – nearly 100 feet wide. Santa Clara itself is an old Spanish town with a beautiful university campus in the centre.

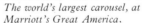

Grape harvest in progress in the sun-soaked Napa Valley

The world's largest carousel, at Marriott's Great America.

On campus is the Mission Santa Clara de Assis, founded in 1777. The present building is a replica of the third mission, built in 1825. The original garden is still preserved, as are three bells donated by the King of Spain.

Drive west along Saratoga Avenue for 5 miles to Saratoga.

Saratoga

A visit to the Paul Masson Champagne and Wine Cellars, on Saratoga Avenue, provides a pleasant introduction to the town. A stroll in the 15-acre Hakkone Gardens on Big Basin Way, with its formal Japanese gardens and a tea room, will make a welcome break.

Head south-west for 4 miles on State Route 9 to Los Gatos.

Los Gatos

Winery tours are also a feature in this town. One mile south on State Route 17 is Novitiate Wines, where a tasting room is open to the public.

Spanish and Victorian architecture blend pleasantly in Old Town on University Avenue.

Shops, restaurants, the California Actors' Theater and craftsmens' studios are some of the attractions. The Los Gatos Museum on Main and Tait Streets has exhibits ranging from local history to art. Children will enjoy riding on the Billy Jones Wildcat Railroad in the park.

Drive north-east on State Route 17 for 17 miles to San José.

San José

Queen of the wine-country, this community is the oldest incorporated city in California. Founded in 1777, it was named Pueblo de San José de Guadalupe. Now it is internationally fêted for the excellence of its table wines.

Approaching the city, near the junction of Interstate 280 and State Route 17 is the baffling Winchester Mystery House (see page 79).

San José is a good place to stay overnight as there is plenty to do and see. Kelley Park offers something for everyone. Happy Hollow is a children's playground, with a baby animal zoo, a treehouse and a model steamboat. The Japanese Friendship Tea Garden with its lanterns is intriguing. Highlight of the park is the San

José Historical Museum, which examines the effects of Indian, Spanish, Mexican and American influences on the Santa Clara Valley. Restored homes, a blacksmith's forge, doctor's office, bank, hotel, print shop and reconstructed stables are on view in the grounds.

Other interesting museums include the Rosicrucian Egyptian Museum in Park Avenue, with a full-size replica of an Egyptian rock tomb, scarabs, paintings, jewels and mummies. San José Museum of Art on Market Street has varying exhibits of traditional and modern art. The New Almaden Mercury Mining Museum on Almaden Road portrays the history of mercury mining, with machinery, equipment and pictures. Indian artefacts are also displayed in the museum.

East of the city, on State Route 130 is Alum Rock Park, nestling in the foothills of the Black Mountain. Walking trails, mineral springs and picnicking areas abound in the 776 acres.

Hotels

BEST WESTERN SANDMAN MOTEL: 2585 Seaboard Av, tel 263 8800. 148 rooms. Moderate.

HYATT SAN JOSÉ: 1740 N 1st St, tel 298 0300. 475 rooms. Expensive.

PEPPER TREE INN: 2112 Monterey Rd, tel 294 1480. 100 rooms. Moderate.

Restaurants

LOU'S VILLAGE: 1465 W San Carlos St, tel 293 4570. Specialities include prime rib, steak, and Eastern seafoods. Children's menu. Expensive.

ORIGINAL JOE'S: 301 S 1st St, tel 292 7030. A family restaurant serving American and Italian food. Inexpensive-moderate.

Leave San José on State Route 82 to join US 101. Drive 43 miles south to San Juan Bautista.

San Juan Bautista

Mission San Juan Bautista, founded in 1797, is the largest of Father Junípero Serra's mission churches. Three of the original five chapel bells remain and the interior walls still bear decorations made by Indian converts.

The old Plaza forms part of a State Historic Park, which includes the Plaza Hotel, built in 1813 for Spanish soldiers, and Castro House, where officials of the Mexican Government had their quarters. A stable, a carriage house, horse-drawn vehicles and a

Plaza Hall – one of several restored buildings in the San Juan Bautista State Historic Park which recall the days of Spanish rule in California

Spanish orchard and garden are other attractive features of the park.

Retrace your steps for 8 miles north along US 101, to take State Route 129 left to Watsonville. Beyond Watsonville take State Route 1 north 19 miles to Santa Cruz. For a detour leave Santa Cruz on State Route 9 driving north through redwood country for 13 miles, then turn left on to State Route 236 which leads to Big Basin Redwoods State Park.

Big Basin Redwoods State Park

Established in 1902, this is the first of the redwood groves to be declared a State Park. The trees are gigantic, some as high as 330 feet with a diameter of 18 feet. Hiking, picnicking and camping are all allowed. There is hunting and fishing in season, swimming in the summer and ice skating, skiing, sledging and tobogganing in winter. Several winter sports centres are nearby.

Return to Santa Cruz south on State Route 9.

Santa Cruz

A bustling resort surrounded by redwoods, Santa Cruz is a mixture of natural beauty and modern entertainment. Santa Cruz Beach Broadwalk is a vast family amusement park with a giant dipper and a cave train. One of Father Serra's missions faces the plaza – Mission Santa Cruz – although the present building is a replica of the original which was founded in 1791.

Da Vinci's painting of the Last Supper is represented with life-size wax figures in an extraordinary reproduction in the Santa Cruz Art League Galleries on Broadway.

On Branciforte Drive, about two miles north of the town, is an area of redwood forest called Mystery Spot, where the laws of gravity appear to be defied. Here a ball will roll *up* a sloping plank and if you climb a hillside it feels like walking on level ground.

Driving north out of Santa Cruz, along the coast is the fascinating Natural Bridge's State Beach, named after the curious surf-carved sandstone arches and rock pools found along this stretch of coast. Monarch butterflies abound here from mid-October to the end of February, when they migrate northwards, some even to Canada.

Hotels

BEST WESTERN TORCH-LITE INN: 500 Riverside Av, tel 426 7575. 38 rooms. Moderate.

DREAM INN: 175 W Cliff Dr, tel 426 4330. 160 rooms. Expensive.

RIO SANDS MOTEL: Between Santa Cruz and Watsonville, at Rio Del Mar Beach, 150 Stephen Rd, tel 688 3207. 50 rooms. Moderate-expensive.

Restaurants

THE COURTYARD RESTAURANT: 4 miles south in Soquel, 2591 Main St, tel 476 2529. Continental cuisine is served in this pleasant garden restaurant overlooking Soquel Creek. Moderate-expensive.

SHADOWBROOK RESTAURANT: 1750 Wharf Rd, tel 475 1511. Set in attractive grounds overlooking creek. A funicular railway takes you down to the dining room. Prime rib and fresh seafood. Expensive.

Return to San Francisco on the scenic, coastal State Route 1. The road follows the coast for 30 miles alongside the sparkling San Mateo Coast State Beaches to San Francisco.

The Yosemite National Park

3 days – 475 miles

San Francisco – Livermore – Merced – Mariposa – Yosemite Valley – Yosemite Village – Big Oak Flat – Columbia – San Francisco

Drive east across the San Francisco Bay – Oakland Bay Bridge and continue through Oakland on Interstate 580 for 42 miles to Livermore.

Livermore

The main town in lush Livermore Valley, this community is surrounded by a delightful country of vineyards and cattle lands, through the midst of which flows the Arroyo del Valle, enhanced by the ancient sycamore trees, some over 200 years old, which grow along its banks. Renowned dry white wines are produced in the local wineries. About three miles to the south of the town are two wineries where you can sample their produce: Wente Brothers and Concannon Vineyards. Both are in Tesla Road.

Five miles south, on Arroyo Road, the famous Del Valle Dam is visible in all its splendour.

About two-and-a-half miles south of Interstate 580, the Lawrence Livermore Laboratory Visitors' Center off Greenville Road has imaginative exhibitions of new energy sources, some in audio-visual presentations.

Continue south on Interstate 580 and join Interstate 5. Drive south for about 30 miles and turn left onto State Route 140. After 35 miles, turn left again on to State Route 99 for Merced.

Merced

This large town, set in the fertile San Joaquin Valley, is well known as a gateway to Yosemite National Park. If you decide to stay overnight here, water sports are

Hotels

BEST WESTERN INN: 1033 Motel Dr, tel 723 2163. 42 rooms. Moderate.

BEST WESTERN PINE CONE INN: 1213 V St, tel 723 3711. 75 rooms. Moderate.

MERCED TRAVELODGE: 2000 E Childs Av, tel 723 3121. 63 rooms. Expensive.

Restaurants

BRANDING IRON: 642 W 16th St, tel 722 1822. Well-prepared dishes, especially steak, lobster and seafood. Children's menu. Expensive.

THE WINE CELLAR: 350 W Main St, tel 723 3796. Countrified restaurant with a varied menu. Children's menu. Moderate-expensive.

available at Yosemite Lake, seven miles to the north-east, and 16 miles south-west is the Merced National Wildlife Refuge.

Continue the approach to the spectacular Yosemite Valley east on State Route 140 for 36 miles to Mariposa.

Mariposa

Gold-rush days are recalled at the Mariposa County History Center. Here you can see a five-stamp mill, horse-drawn vehicles, mining equipment and replicas of a print shop, a schoolroom, a miner's cabin, an apothecary's shop and an Indian village.

The oldest courthouse in California, built in 1854, is still in use here. This two-storey, white pine building was constructed with wooden pegs. The quaint, square clock tower houses an old clock which was brought to California via Cape Horn.

Some distance to the east of the town is the spectacular sequoia stand of Mariposa Grove. It is reached through Wawona by taking the Wawona Tunnel out of Yosemite Valley. The oldest redwood, Grizzly Giant, has a base diameter of nearly 35 feet, a girth of almost 100 feet and is over 200 feet high. You can be driven through a tunnel in the base of the California Tree. Trips are organised to the grove every day from Yosemite Valley. A museum displays exhibits of giant redwood and is open to coincide with summer season tram tours.

Continue east for another 40 miles on State Route 140 and cross Yosemite Valley over the road bridge.

Cowboys roping a steer at the Livermore Rodeo

SCALE 20.5 MILES TO 1 INCH

KILOMETRES

©AMERICAN AUTOMOBILE ASSOCIATION MCMLXXXI

84

Yosemite Valley

Carved by glaciers, this mile-wide valley is flanked by sheer granite cliffs and imposing mountain peaks. Meadows and forests carpet the valley floor and the Merced River threads through the seven-mile length of the valley. Towering over 7,500 feet above sea level, El Capitan is the most spectacular western outcrop, with a 3,500-foot sheer single block of glinting perpendicular granite. Half Dome, at almost 9,000 feet, dominates the eastern end of the valley, with Sentinel Dome and North Dome in attendance. Gigantic waterfalls tumble over the tops of the cliffs, most amazing of which is Yosemite Falls. Cascading in two falls over the north wall, Upper Yosemite Fall has a drop equal to nine Niagara's – 1,430 feet! Immediately below, Lower Yosemite Fall drops a mere 320 feet. Ribbon Fall, at 1,612 feet is the highest single fall. Other spectacular falls include misty Bridalveil, Nevada, Illilouette and Vernal. At their fullest in May and fairly abundant up to mid-July, the falls are virtually dry during the rest of the summer. The approach from Mariposa offers splendid views of the Three Brothers – a trio of peaks over 6,000 feet high, as well as El Capitan.

At the head of the valley is Yosemite Village.

Yosemite Village

Packed with tourist attractions, it is still the drama of the surrounding mountain flanks and giant forests which gives the village its appeal. The most compelling viewpoint is the lofty 7,000-foot Glacier Point which gives a panoramic view of the High Sierras, including El Capitan and

Yosemite Falls, in Yosemite National Park, has a total fall from crest to valley floor of 2,425 feet

Half Dome, and of Upper Yosemite, Nevada and Vernal Falls backed by snowy mountains. Reached by a sinuous path through red fir and pine forests, the road is the route used on daily organised trips to Glacier Point from the village. Unfortunately it is closed in winter.

The visitors' centre, however, is open all year. Audio-visual programmes explaining the formation of the valley are shown here and maps and general information are available. A free daily shuttle bus service operates through the valley and an open tram tours the valley in summer. There are plenty of camp sites and numerous hotels and restaurants. Children may be left in a

supervised play area – at nearby Curry Village in the summer or at Ski Tots Club at Badgers Pass in winter.

At Happy Isles Nature Center, just south of the village, you can take a nature walk with a naturalist during summer. Walks last from half an hour to a whole day.

Other activities include mountaineering, with guided climbs; guided tours on horseback; hiking trails and bicycles may be rented from Curry Village or

The magnificent view from Glacier Point, 3,254-feet above the Merced River and the Yosemite Valley in Yosemite National Park

Yosemite Lodge. In winter, skiing instruction is available at Badger's Pass Ski Center and there is an outdoor skating rink near Curry Village. It is a good idea to begin your visit at the Visitor Center, and pick up the free newsletter, *Yosemite Guide.*

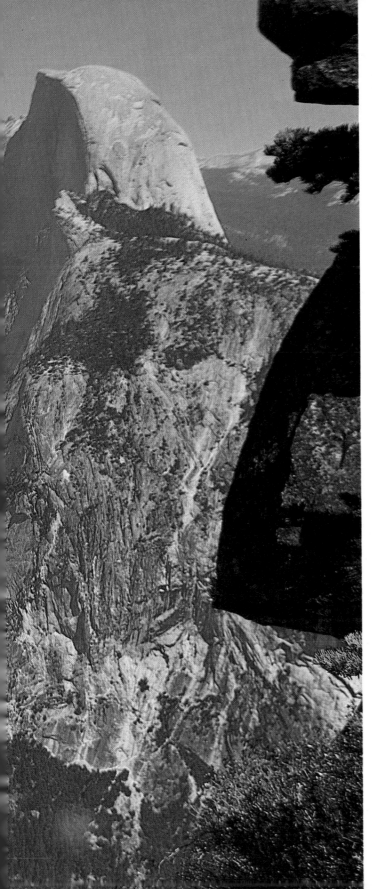

The original Fire-Engine Station in Columbia State Historic Park

As you leave Yosemite Village along North Valley Road, you will see to the south of the river the 6,000-foot pinnacles of the Cathedral Spires.

Hotels

AHWAHNEE HOTEL: ¾ mile E beyond Park Headquarters, tel 373 4171. 121 rooms. Expensive.

CURRY VILLAGE: 2 miles E and across the Merced River from Park Headquarters, tel 373 4171. 600 rooms. Inexpensive-moderate.

YOSEMITE LODGE: ¾ mile W of Park Headquarters, at foot of Yosemite Falls, tel 373 4171. 474 rooms. Moderate.

From the north entrance to Yosemite Valley, take New Big Oak Flat Road for 8 miles to Crane Flat. Here join the beautiful Big Oak Flat Highway – State Route 120 – for a 41-mile drive through dramatic, mountainous country to Big Oak Flat.

Big Oak Flat

Originally called Savage Diggings, after James Savage who founded the town in 1850 as a goldmining centre, the present name was inspired by a vast valley oak which grew in the centre of town. Two pieces of the original oak preserved in a monument on the site are all that remain of the tree. The only other remnants of the old gold-rush town are a few old stone and brick buildings.

Continue west on State Route 120 and join State Route 49. After 13 miles, turn right for Jamestown and Sonora. From Jamestown, follow an unclassified road for one mile to Columbia.

Columbia

Once one of the most important goldmining towns in California, Columbia is picturesquely placed in the foothills of the Sierra Nevada. Here gold was extracted from sand and gravel in stream-beds and around 87 million dollars in gold was extracted between 1850 and 1880.

Restored in appearance to the days of the gold rush, Columbia State Historic Park has buildings which include saloons, a barber's shop, a bank, a school, a newspaper office, the famous Wells Fargo Express Company, and the City Hotel, which offers tours and accommodation. An old theatre presents stage shows, and stage-coach rides are available daily in summer and during fine weekends in winter.

Hotels

COLUMBIA GEM MOTEL: 3 miles N of Sonora, on Columbia Hwy, tel 532 4508. 12 rooms. Moderate.

COLUMBIA INN MOTEL: Adjacent to Columbia State Historic Park, tel 533 0446. 24 rooms. Moderate.

Restaurant

CITY HOTEL DINING ROOM: in Columbia State Historic Park, in City Hotel, tel 532 1479. Elegantly furnished restaurant serving continental cuisine. Also 9 hotel rooms. Expensive.

Return to Sonora, then continue west on State Route 49 then State Route 120 for 57 miles to Manteca. Here take Interstate 205 for 22 miles to Livermore. Drive the last 42 miles west on Interstate 580 to San Francisco.

In the high season, when the village is overcrowded, those intending to stay overnight should make a detour to Tuolumne Meadows. These high alpine meadows overlook the valley from the north and are accessible during summer along the spectacular Tioga Pass – a mountain road of hairpin bends. Lakes and vast stands of pine, overshadowed by mountains, complete the attraction of a camp site here, where meals are served under canvas.

San Francisco

Most Americans have never been to San Francisco, yet a national poll found that, above all other cities, 'the cool gray City of Gold' was where Americans would live given the choice. No other town exerts such an attraction as San Francisco.

It is a small town, with barely 750,000 inhabitants, but its aura is one of Big City. The people are said to be the best dressed in America, the business area around Union Square equals Paris for smartness, the shops are equal to those in New York for style. San Francisco is chic, sophisticated, enchantingly beautiful, and touchingly eccentric, with its immaculate story-book houses clinging to the steep slopes down which clanging, rather absurd cable-

cars hurtle as though the streets were a fairground.

Allied to the quaint charm of her architecture, San Francisco's special philosophy of tolerance must be responsible for part of her charisma. Sophisticated the city may be, but not conservative.

In 1906 an earthquake destroyed much of San Francisco. Jack London, the author, wrote in a newspaper dispatch from the scene – 'the City of San Francisco . . . is no more.' The town which fell was a haven for gangsters and whores, vigilante groups and organised crime. But in its place rose the new San Francisco, a city of culture and charm.

▶ *The Golden Gate Bridge, which spans the mouth of San Francisco Bay, has an overall length of 8,981 feet*

▼ *The two sides of San Francisco; the Victorian gingerbread houses of the old city, and the high-rise blocks of the new*

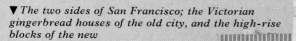

One of the most enduring charms of this sophisticated, literate and wonderfully resourceful city, which undulates like a roller coaster between the Pacific Ocean and the Golden Gate, is that few among its 663,500 inhabitants can make up their minds how many ups and downs there are in San Francisco. Some say 40, others more. What is not in dispute is that San Francisco stands on seven lofty hills, and the ripples that flow from them can suddenly confront the unsuspecting motorist with a terrifyingly steep gradient or a series of tight bends. The city claims to have the crookedest street in the world – Lombard Street – and what driver would doubt it as he slaloms headlong into ten tight S turns down towards the Bay.

Such contours present massive transport problems for the city, but unlike Los Angeles, San Francisco has not solved them by building elevated highways over the rooftops. Although there are major fast roads cutting through parts of the city, there are also forlorn sections of multi-lane freeways which end abruptly in the middle of nowhere. They were started and never finished as the planners wisely concluded that San Francisco should go on living with its uniquely practical transportation system – the cable

SAN FRANCISCO

car – as long as its built-in tourist attraction and its modest running costs allowed.

The cable cars, of course, intrude into the motorists' right of way at almost every turn. Like tramline vehicles elsewhere, their lack of maneouverability can make them a serious hazard to a traffic-packed street – particularly at junctions.

Inevitably there are collisions, especially when a cable car has to run down a one in five gradient and stop at a busy crossing at the bottom. Surprisingly they are very safe. Each car has four separate braking devices – one even that needs a welding crew to unclamp – and although the system is antiquated, the cars themselves are built to a high standard of modern safety.

Each car is pulled at 9½ miles an hour by a series of subterranean cables winched from a control centre. The Cable Car Barn, at Washington and Mason Streets, houses the huge winding machinery. The museum attached allows visitors a glimpse of the system's early days. Although much of the city was destroyed seven times by fire and earthquake, the cable car transport has survived for over 100 years.

It was in 1869 that a London-born wire-rope manufacturer and engineer called Andrew Hallidie hit on the idea of providing the city with a means of transport appropriate to its special needs. He had watched a team of four horses struggle up a steep San Francisco slope pulling a heavily-laden cart. The horses faltered, slipped on the cobbles and, unable to hold the weight behind them, tumbled back down the hill out of control.

It took Hallidie four years to devise a practical alternative to horsepower, and on 2 August 1873, he launched the first cable car down Nob Hill's east side. Soon about 10½ miles of San Francisco's streets were covered by three routes, and little has changed since then. The cable cars have even survived the ravages of the post-war developers when the lines might have been ripped up, together with much else the 1906 earthquake had spared. By 1964 the United States Government had become the system's guardian angel, by preserving it as a historic landmark. Since then, it has been a priority on every tourist itinerary.

There are, of course, alternative means of public transport in the city. Buses and conventional trams provide an efficient surface service, and there is the controversial subway system linking the communities across the Bay. Sleek and efficient, BART (for Bay Area Rapid Transit) is viewed with profound suspicion by many San Franciscans, particularly since a disastrous fire in one of the carriages several years ago. They prefer to drive and have come to terms with the special demands the city makes on motorists. As most cars have automatic gearboxes and impeccably efficient brakes, the hills are no longer a problem to residents or visitors, as long as they remember to park with the wheel tucked well into the kerb to prevent the car from rolling.

San Francisco's most attractive areas are linked by a well-signposted 49-mile scenic drive. There is much to see. The Golden Gate Bridge, Chinatown, Japan Center, Fisherman's Wharf, and, of course, the high-class range of hotels, restaurants and shops in the eight-square-mile heart of the city. It has more than 50,000 hotel rooms and has built twenty new hotels over the past ten years. Some of the finest views are from the bars and restaurants found at the top of the

▲ *Chinatown Wax Museum recreates scenes from the early days of Chinese settlement in California*

◀ *Bay Area Rapid Transit System, or BART, a luxurious high-speed rail network, is San Francisco's answer to traffic congestion*

▶ *The controversial shape of the Transamerica Pyramid in Chinatown*

▼ *Lombard Street, called 'the crookedest street in the world', descends a 40-degree slope in a series of landscaped curves*

city's famous hotels, such as the Top of the Mark in the Mark Hopkins Hotel on Nob Hill, Hugo's One-up in the Hyatt Hotel in Union Square, and the Equinon at the Hyatt Regency in the Embarcadero Center, which is the only revolving restaurant in San Francisco.

A cheaper way to see the rooftops of San Francisco is to climb 300-foot Russian Hill, or Telegraph Hill, also 300 foot high, which offers a viewpoint a further 210 feet up from the top of the Coit Memorial Tower. This column commemorates one of San Francisco's most respected public services – the volunteer fire-men, who, in one disastrous period of two years in the last century, fought six devastating fires in the city. They also had to stand by impotently during the 1906 earthquake, when the water mains broke and no water was available for the hoses. The fires raged for three days. The earthquake and its aftermath claimed 600 victims, destroying around 28,000 buildings and wiping out the entire north-east side of the city.

The next half century saw the destruction by the developers of most of the buildings that survived the earthquakes, but since San Francisco's vigorous re-storation programme got under way in the 1950s, more than 7,000 houses have been restored. Some of

San Francisco's more flourishing craftsmen these days are the painters and designers at work fashion-ing and building replicas of the 19th-century stone and wood façades in an effort to recreate the original appearance of the houses. This love affair with the past is not just an indulgence. The relaxed character of the city, and its ineffable appeal, relies on its ability to absorb progress without allowing modern designs to overwhelm it. Controversy is easy to raise over any changes in San Francisco's skyline.

The 34-million dollar Transamerica Corpor-ation's pyramid-shaped building, stretching 853 feet into the sky and dwarfing the other giants around it, has never quite been accepted. The planners tried to soften the impact by planting a half-acre of redwood trees on its east side, but the city still argues about whether such a bold shape should have a place in San Francisco.

Another row developed over the new St Mary's Catholic Cathedral, which some people say looks like a washing machine agitator. Standing on the site of its predecessor, destroyed in 1962 in a fire on Cathedral Hill, its design has provoked argument for more than ten years. It is made of Italian marble and contains a baldachin of aluminium and gold, a large

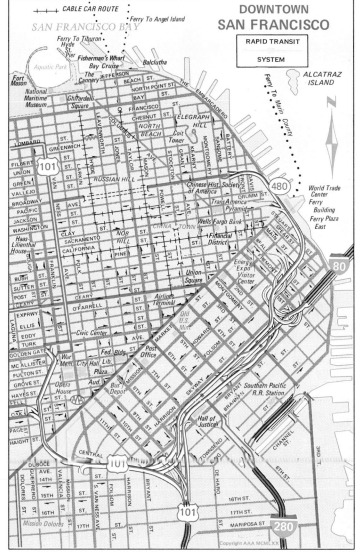

SAN FRANCISCO

mosaic and a Ruffati organ. The then Archbishop of San Francisco had no doubts; when the cathedral was finished he presented the architect with a tiny silver cable car. It was the ultimate honour!

No such recognition was given to San Francisco's first 'architect', Father Juniperio Serra, for providing it with one of the first six of the 21 Spanish Missions he built on the California coast between the years 1769 and 1823.

Mission Dolores opened in October 1776, the same year the first white settlement was established. It still stands at 16th and Dolores Street, though now only the church and the cemetery garden remain intact. The Mission, like so many others created by the Franciscan friars, became a resting place and victuals storehouse for the missionaries. When Colonel Juna Batista de Anza established a Spanish military post on the southern shore of the Golden Gate (the entrance to the bay) in the same year just a few miles away, it was inevitable that a trail should be marked out between the two posts. It encouraged visits from traders and this led to the growth of the community and the establishment of the town of Yerba Buena. Its name was later changed into San Francisco. The town had only about 100 inhabitants until in the heady days of the gold rush thousands of prospectors

were suddenly attracted to it. By 1861, San Francisco's population had passed the 10,000 mark and though access was confined mainly to the sea, the arrival of the Trans Continental railroad in 1869 changed all that. The track opened up the floodgates to the west coast, and San Francisco became besieged with prospectors.

Signs of the city's pioneering days can be found in a stretch of Union Street, called Cow Hollow. Here, just over 100 years ago, dairy herds grazed. Now its nooks and crannies are full of charming specialist shops and galleries, with flower-filled courtyards beckoning the visitor into another age.

Similar narrow streets have been preserved in Jackson Square, part of the official historic district of the city, and near the eastern end of Jackson Street.

Union Square, which is not connected with Union Street (it is not even in the vicinity), is the core of the commercial activity of San Francisco. It is flanked by the fashionable shopping streets of Powell, Post, Geary and Stockton. Bursting with fine merchandise and glittering façades, the square was one of the first in the post-war boom to be revitalised.

Fashionable shops can also be found in the new-style shopping malls, such as the Embarcadero Center near the waterfront – an unobtrusive

▲ *Mission Dolores, believed to be the oldest building in San Francisco, was built long before the city which now surrounds it*

◀ *The Marina Small Craft Harbour on Marina Boulevard, with the dome of the Palace of Fine Arts behind*

▲ *Just across the Golden Gate Bridge is delightful Sausolito, a focal point for artists attracted by the marine setting and unusual architecture*

◀ *Formerly a fruit cannery, The Cannery has been transformed into an attractive network of small shops and art galleries*

▼ *Pier 39, adjoining Fisherman's Wharf, is one of San Francisco's modern schemes for turning derelict areas into attractive and useful complexes*

treasurehouse of fine living. The waterfront has many attractive features. Fisherman's Wharf, one of San Francisco's more famous tourist haunts, is just a few minutes walk from the much more stylish surroundings of Ghirardelli Square, a building (not a square at all) where once a thriving chocolate factory produced a famous brand of chocolate. One of the attractions is to see the chocolate still being made – but purely for the benefit of tourists. For Ghirardelli Square is a complex of galleries, restaurants and speciality shops which, like the new Covent Garden in London, attracts young street entertainers anxious to find a place to play and perform before an audience. Its success has led to several similar complexes being set up.

The Cannery, a few blocks from Fisherman's Wharf, was once a fruit-canning factory. It has more specialised shops but, like Pier 39, rivals Fisherman's Wharf as a tourist attraction. Pier 39 opened only in 1978, and also provides a platform for young musicians, jugglers and such likes.

With more than 2,600 restaurants to choose from, San Francisco can serve up any kind of food in the world. Chinatown, the largest Chinese community in the West, extends for 24 blocks and houses a restaurant every few steps. Japan Center has developed in line with the rapid growth of the Japanese community in the city. Bounded by Post, Geary, Laguna and Fillmore streets, it has become a cultural and commercial showplace, with restaurants, shops, theatres and hotels. But while the Chinese tend to stay within their township, the Japanese are seen all over San Francisco. Often the second language at tourist places is Japanese! And they are even prouder of the city than the indigenous white resident. Their loyalty and enthusiasm is a tribute to San Francisco's insidious charms. Its qualities have drawn artists and writers, inspired eulogies and epigrams and created a

myth that often does not do justice to the reality.

Somerset Maugham considered it 'the most civilised city in America', but in the 1980s it is its tolerance, and its lack of frenzy, which make it so memorable. In that sense it is more European than any other city in America – even Boston, which in some ways is more familiarly British.

The British have several practical reminders of home, like the Pelican Inn on State Route 1, less than 20 minutes from the Golden Gate Bridge. It specialises in a selection of genuine English beers, served in a 16th-century-style panelled bar with a dartboard, low beams, shining brasses and a clientele as near to the real thing as the circumstances allow. It looks right from the outside, too – a beamed, white-painted cottage, which has become accepted as part of the San Francisco scene.

Straddling the entrance to the bay, and connecting Marin County and the north, the Golden Gate Bridge is disappointingly painted rust red. When it opened in 1937, it was the longest single-span suspension bridge in the world. Its one-and-a-half-mile-long main span, 220 feet above the water (to allow for the passage of large ocean-going steamers), carries rush-hour commuter traffic morning and night to the dormitory towns of Sausalito, San Rafael and Tiburon (whose winding, wooded streets are reminiscent of villages in parts of France or Cornwall). The two massive towers, the highest ever built, rise 746 feet above the water. Overall, the bridge, which in the 1970s was the top tourist attraction in America, is 8,981 feet long and collects a modest toll for city-bound traffic only, apparently on the basis that, as Rudyard Kipling said of San Francisco ''tis hard to leave', and that those who drive out of it, will surely come back! The trip out of San Francisco through the rainbow-fringed tunnel at the north end can become part of a circular tour which takes in the

other two main bridges across the Bay – the Richmond–San Rafael Bridge to Richmond, and the 8¼-mile-long, double-tiered San Francisco–Oakland Bay Bridge.

This connects with the East Bay cities of Oakland, Alameda and Berkeley. The bridge goes through a double-decked tunnel at Yerba Buena Island which connects with Treasure Island, a United States Naval Station. Though both bridges cope well with traffic, in rush hours they tend to be overloaded, so ferry services across the Bay are increasingly patronised by commuters as well as visitors.

Angel Island, a former army stronghold, has become a popular weekend retreat for many San Franciscans since 1962, when this 740-acre wildlife preserve was last used as an enlistment and discharge centre. The army huts still stand, but are shuttered and silent. No cars are allowed on the island. During the height of the summer, the ferries run all week, but only at weekends for the rest of the year. Nonetheless the frequency of the ferries allows a full-day's picnicking or exploring on the many trails and bikepaths.

The busiest ferry route across the Bay ends with a guided tour of Alcatraz, the notorious prison fortress which for nearly 100 years incarcerated America's most dangerous criminals. Here Al Capone, Machine-gun Kelly and the Birdman were some of the better-known inmates. Only three were believed to have got away, though whether they perished in the icy waters of the bay or successfully vanished into obscurity will never be known. It was, however, far too costly to run. On 21 March 1963, the last remaining 27 convicts in handcuffs, leg irons and waist chains were taken off Alcatraz. The prison was shut down, and it was another ten years before it was reopened as a grim museum. Today it serves as an ironic reminder of the harsh conditions men endured for much of their lives within sight of one of the most civilised cities on earth.

Now the queues stretch for hundreds of yards for each sailing to the island, even though visitors are warned that the steep climbs and stone steps, and the mile-long walk around the perimeter road of the prison are arduous and demanding. Like the Golden Gate Bridge, it has become one of the great tourist attractions of the United States.

▲ *The cable cars of San Francisco first ran in 1873, and are a leading tourist attraction – half the passengers are invariably tourists paying just for the roller coaster ride. In the distance is Alcatraz Island, once the site of America's most notorious penitentiary*

◀ *The Conservatory in Golden Gate Park in which tropical plants are kept, and where there is always a stunning show of flowers*

San Francisco Directory

HOTELS

The hotels and restaurants listed here are either recommended by the American Automobile Association (AAA) or have been selected because they are of interest to tourists. As a rough guide to cost they have been classified as either expensive, moderate or inexpensive. Hotels, unless otherwise stated, all have private bathrooms and colour television.

BARRETT: 501 Post St, tel 441 7100. 140 rooms. 14-storey building. Conference rooms. Baby-sitting. Café. Moderate.

BECK'S MOTOR LODGE: 2222 Market St, tel 467 8811. 56 rooms. Sun-deck. Restaurant nearby. Coin laundry. Moderate.

BEST WESTERN AMERICANIA: 121 7th St, tel 626 0200. 145 rooms. Meeting rooms. Free parking. Pool. Sauna. Moderate.

BEST WESTERN EL RANCHO: 1100 El Camino Real, tel 588 2912. 250 rooms and 14 self-catering apartments. Inexpensive.

BEST WESTERN KYOTO INN: 1800 Sutter St, tel 921 4000. 125 rooms. Family rooms. Steam-baths. Moderate.

CABLE MOTOR INN: 1450 Lombard St, tel 673 0691. 72 rooms. Colour TV. Sun-deck.

Family rooms. Expensive.

CAPRI MOTEL: 2015 Greenwich St, tel 346 4667. 45 rooms. Shower-baths. Moderate.

CHANCELLOR HOTEL: 433 Powell St, tel 362 2004. 150 rooms. Valet parking. Dining-room. Moderate.

COW HOLLOW MOTOR INN: 2190 Lombard St, tel 921 5800. 60 rooms. Adjacent coffee-shop. Moderate.

EL CORTEZ HOTEL: 550 Geary St, tel 775 5000. 170 rooms.

Valet parking. Restaurant. Cocktails. Moderate.

FAIRMONT HOTEL AND TOWER: 950 Mason St, tel 772 5000. 595 rooms. Top name entertainment. Expensive.

FOUR SEASONS CLIFT HOTEL: 495 Geary St, tel 775 4700. 405 rooms. Valet parking. Wheelchair rooms. Shower-baths. Expensive.

HOLIDAY INN-AIRPORT: 245 S Airport Blvd, tel 589 7200. 332 rooms. Pool. Restaurant and coffee-shop. Moderate.

HOLIDAY INN-FINANCIAL DISTRICT: 750 Kearny St, tel 433 6600. 557 rooms. Garage. Rooftop pool. Café. Entertainment. Expensive.

HYATT ON UNION SQUARE: 345 Stockton St, tel 398 1234. 710 rooms. In-room movies. Valet parking. Disco. Restaurant. Butler service. Expensive.

MARK HOPKINS HOTEL: 1 Nob Hill Circle, tel 392 3434. 366 rooms. Pay garage. Excellent rooms. Expensive.

MIYAKO HOTEL: 1625 Post St, tel 922 3200. 200 rooms. Japanese décor. Beauty shops. Barber. Restaurant and café. Sauna. Expensive.

PACIFICA PLAZA: 501 Post St, tel 441 7100. 140 rooms. Pay garage. Restaurant. Expensive.

QUALITY INN: 2775 Van Ness Av, tel 928 9500. 140 rooms. Meeting rooms. Garage. Restaurant. Expensive.

RAMADA INN-FISHERMAN'S WHARF: 590 Bay St, tel 885 4700. 231 rooms. Pool. Restaurant and café. Dancing and entertainment. Expensive.

RAPHAEL: 386 Geary St, tel 986 2000. 150 rooms. Shower-baths. Restaurant. Library. Expensive.

ROYAL PACIFIC MOTOR INN: 661 Broadway, tel 781 6661. 62 rooms. Shower-baths. Moderate.

ST FRANCIS HOTEL: 335 Powell St, tel 397 7000. 1,200 rooms. Deluxe rooms. Valet parking. Entertainment and dancing. Drug-store. Restaurant. Expensive.

SAN FRANCISCO HILTON: 330 O'Farrell St, tel 771 1400. 1,800 rooms. Pool. Sun-deck. Penthouse suites. Entertainment. Expensive.

SEAL ROCK INN: 545 Point Lobos Av, tel 752 8000. 27 rooms. Comb-baths. Small pool. Moderate.

SIR FRANCIS DRAKE HOTEL: 450 Powell St, tel 392 7755. 415 rooms. Movies. Dancing nightly. Pay garage. Expensive.

VAGABOND MOTOR HOTEL-DOWNTOWN: 2550 Van Ness Av, tel 776 7500. 133 rooms. Suites. Small pool. Nearby restaurant. Expensive.

WHARF MOTEL: 2601 Mason St, tel 673 7411. 50 rooms. Coin laundry. Shower-baths. Moderate.

RESTAURANTS

ALEXIS RESTAURANT: 1001 California St, tel 885 6400. Russian and French dishes served amid Byzantine décor. Cocktails. Expensive.

ALFRED'S: 886 Broadway, tel 781 7058. Popular restaurant with a mainly steak menu. Specialities include veal piccata and fresh salmon. Moderate.

AMELIO'S: 1630 Powell St, tel 397 4339. Intimate dining in elegant surroundings. Mainly French and Italian dishes. House desserts. Background music. Moderate.

THE BEGINNING: 2020 Filmore St, tel 563 9948. Deep South menu with children's portions Plantation theme décor. Moderate.

BENIHANA OF TOKYO: 740 Taylor St, tel 771 8414. Japanese cuisine and hibachi-style cooking. Strict dress code. Moderate.

BLUE FOX: 659 Merchant St, tel 981 1177. High-class restaurant with three dining-rooms. Specialities include duckling flambé aux cerises noires and loin of lamb Antoinette. Expensive.

THE BUSH GARDEN: 598 Bush St, tel 986 1600. Japanese restaurant with picturesque pond, waterfall and footbridge. Background music. Expensive.

CANLIS RESTAURANT: 950 Mason St, tel 772 5233. Continental cuisine, predominantly seafood and steaks. Children's menu. Expensive.

CARNELIAN ROOM: 555 California St, tel 433 7500. Fine views of the city and excellent French cuisine. 18th-century décor. Moderate.

THE CASTAGNOLA: 286 Jefferson St, tel 776 5015. Large menu with seafood specialities and children's portions. Valet parking at lunchtimes. Sea views. Inexpensive.

CHARLEY BROWN'S: 1550 Bayshore Hwy, tel 697 6907. Steak and lobster specialities. Sunday brunch. Entertainment. Inexpensive.

ERNIE'S: 847 Montgomery St, tel 397 5969. Top-class Continental cuisine, making this restaurant the haunt of gourmets. Superb wine list. Expensive.

HUGO'S MARKET: 1333 Old Bayshore Hwy, tel 342 7741. Varied menu and extensive salad bar. Dancing. Moderate.

LEHR'S GREENHOUSE: Canterbury Hotel, 740 Sutter St, tel 474 6478. Pleasant garden setting. Salad buffet. Moderate.

ONDINE RESTAURANT: 558 Bridgeway, Sausalito, tel 332 0792. Fine views for diners. French speciality dishes. Expensive.

SCHROEDER'S CAFE: 240 Front St, tel 421 4778. Long-established German restaurant. Moderate.

TRADER VIC'S: 20 Cosmos Pl, tel 776 2232. Valet parking. Continental and Polynesian dishes. Moderate.

VENETO RESTAURANT: 389 Bay St, tel 986 4553. Four dining-rooms serving mainly Italian dishes. Rare dolls on display. Cocktails. Moderate.

YAMATO RESTAURANT: 717 California St, tel 397 3456. Fine Japanese food in delightful surroundings. Children's menu. Cocktails. Moderate.

TRANSPORT

SAN FRANCISCO INTERNATIONAL AIRPORT: 16 miles S near San Mateo, on US 101. Over 25 domestic and international airlines work out of the airport and there is a direct flight to the majority of large American cities. Buses and coaches ply regularly between the airport and the city, the journey takes approximately 45 minutes, longer when traffic is heavy. Both bus and coach prices are a lot cheaper than taxis. Main operators are: Airporter, corner of Taylor and Ellis Sts, tel 673 2432; Sam Trans; Greyhound.

LIMOUSINES: Major companies are: Associated Limousines, tel 824 2660; Airport Limousines, tel 595 3636; Holiday Limousines, tel 447 3129.

TAXIS: Journeys by taxi can prove expensive, so it is best to enquire prices before setting out on a long trip. Major operators are: DeSoto Cab, tel 673 1414; Luxor Cab, tel 552 4040; Veteran's Cab, tel 552 1300; Yellow Cab, tel 626 2345.

CAR HIRE: Yellow Pages has a comprehensive section on car hire. However, the major companies tend to give the best and most flexible service, especially between the city and the airport. Useful numbers are: Avis Rent-A-Car, tel 885 5011; Budget Rent-A-Car, tel 928 7863; Dollar Rent-A-Car Systems, tel 673 2137; Hertz Rent-A-Car, tel 771 2200.

CABLE CARS: operated by the San Francisco Municipal Railway, tel 673-MUNI. 39 cable cars (often called 'grips') operate over the three different types of track.

THE BAY AREA RAPID TRANSIT SYSTEM: tel 788-BART. A to and fro service from San Francisco to the East Bay via a tunnel.

GOLDEN GATE FERRIES: a frequent service to Marin County, with routes linking Sausalito and Larkspur from the terminal at Market St. For further information tel 332 6600. Other operators are: Tiburon Ferry, tel 546 2815; Blue & Gold Fleet, tel 781 7877; Gold Coast Fleet, tel 775 9108; Red & White Fleet, tel 546 2815.

RAIL SERVICES: AMTRAK, USA's interstate railroad, provides shuttle buses from the city centre ticket office (at 1st and Mission Sts) to main rail terminal. All-inclusive tours to many destinations are also offered by AMTRAK, tel 648 3850 (Freephone).

TOURING INFORMATION

CALIFORNIA STATE AUTOMOBILE ASSOCIATION: 150 Van Ness Av, tel 565 2012.

AUTO TAPE TOURS: 433 Mason St. Hertz excursions to Monterey.

GUIDED CITY WALKS: Chinese Heritage Walks, tel 986 1822; walks including City Hall, fire department and civic centre, tel 558 3949; Golden Gate Park Walks, tel 543 4664 (May–October); Heritage Walks, tel 441 3046.

SAN FRANCISCO CONVENTION AND VISITORS' BUREAU: 1390 Market St, tel 626 5500.

SHOPPING

CHINATOWN: As you would expect, nearly all shops specialise in products of the Orient. The many items sold include porcelain, ivory, teak goods and bamboo furniture. Location of the Chinatown Gate is the junction of Bush and Grant Sts.

COST PLUS: A precinct at Fisherman's Wharf where all goods are imported and range from 'joke' items to the strange and exotic.

EMBARCADERO CENTER: off Market and Sacramento Sts. A specially built complex of shops and offices designed on three levels. The area features shops, houses, hotels and galleries interspersed throughout with sculptures and tapestries.

GHIRARDELLI SQUARE: A small precinct of restaurants and shops built on the former site of a chocolate company.

KINTETSU SHOPPING CENTER: in the Japan Center, bounded by Post, Geary and Fillmore Sts. Enclosed two-level shopping arcade that features Japanese flower arranging, pearl culture and ceramics demonstrations.

SUTTER STREET: N of Union Sq. Trendy boutiques, stylish furniture, haute couture, fine arts and unusual accessory shops.

UNION STREET: between Franklin and Steiner Sts. Antique shops and boutiques housed in Victorian buildings.

MUSEUMS

ASIAN ART MUSEUM: Golden Gate Pk. Large collection of bronzes, ceramics, jades and paintings from the East.

CALIFORNIA ACADEMY OF SCIENCES: Golden Gate Pk, tel 752 8268. Huge exhibition complex. Cowell Hall features dinosaurs, the history of man is traced in Wattis Hall and many fishes at the Steinhart Aquarium. A major building in the park is the Morrison Planetarium.

CALIFORNIA HISTORICAL SOCIETY: 2090 Jackson St. A changing exhibition of paintings and photographs housed in a Victorian mansion.

CHINESE HISTORICAL SOCIETY: 17 Adler Pl. Specialist exhibition charting Chinese development in America.

CHINATOWN WAX MUSEUM: 601 Grant Av. Historical events depicted in over thirty colourful tableaux.

GUINNESS MUSEUM OF WORLD RECORDS: 235 Jefferson St, tel 771 9890. Contents act as evidence for the now world-famous book of the biggest, highest, widest etc.

JOSEPHINE D RANDALL JR MUSEUM: 199 Museum Way. Natural history and model railway exhibitions plus features on Indian life in California and specialist seismographic equipment.

LELAND STANFORD JR MUSEUM: Stanford University in Palo Alto. Oriental and Renaissance art, Rodin bronzes and Egyptian antiquities.

MEXICAN MUSEUM. 1855 Folsom St. Rotating displays of early and contemporary Mexican art.

NATIONAL MARITIME MUSEUM: Aquatic Pk, Polk St, tel 556 8177. Water transport displays from the 1800s to the present day. Featured is the *Balclutha* (pier 43), a museum ship originally launched in Scotland in 1886.

OAKLAND MUSEUM: Tenth and Oak Sts in Oakland, tel 273 3401. A complex of gardens and galleries reflecting the history, ecology and art of California.

OLD US MINT: at Fifth and Mission Sts. The building itself is a fine example of Revival architecture. Displays include nuggets, medals and coins plus a pyramid of gold bullion valued at over $1 million.

PRESIDIO ARMY MUSEUM: at Lincoln Blvd and Funston Av. Displays cover more than 100

years of San Franciscan military history.

RIPLEY'S BELIEVE-IT-OR-NOT MUSEUM: 175 Jefferson St, Fisherman's Wharf. Bizarre oddities collected by the cartoonist Robert L Ripley. Items range from the smallest violin in the world to a two-headed goat.

SAN FRANCISCO FIRE DEPARTMENT MUSEUM: 655 Presidio Av, tel 558 3949. Over 100 years of fire-fighting history depicted through relics and equipment.

WAX MUSEUM: 145 Jefferson St, Fisherman's Wharf, tel 885 4975. San Francisco's version of Madame Tussaud's featuring Chamber of Horrors, Hall of Fame and replicas of Tutankhamen's treasures.

WELLS FARGO HISTORY ROOM: Wells Fargo Bank, 420 Montgomery St. Stamps and relics from 1848 onwards plus an original stagecoach.

WINE MUSEUM: 633 Beach St. The Christian Brothers' collection traces the history of wine back to Roman and Greek times. Many rare drinking vessels.

SPORT

CANDLESTICK PARK: 8 miles S off Route 101. The baseball home of the San Francisco Giants and football venue for the San Francisco 49ers. For baseball tickets tel 467 8000; for football tickets tel 468 2249.

COW PALACE: at Geneva Av and Santos St. The largest indoor stadium west of Chicago. Tennis, indoor soccer and wrestling are among the many sports, plus rodeos and trade fairs.

GOLF: Courses include Olympic Club (listed in the top ten American courses), Lincoln Park and Harding Park.

OAKLAND-ALAMEDA COUNTY COLISEUM COMPLEX: via Nimitz Freeway across the bay, tel 776 9404. Indoor arena, hall and stadium that holds 52,000 people. Home of the Golden State Warriors, San Francisco's professional basketball team.

PLACES OF INTEREST

ALCATRAZ ISLAND: $1\frac{1}{4}$ miles offshore in San Francisco Bay, tel 546 2805. Former site of a famous maximum-security penitentiary. Two-hour guided tours leave from Fisherman's Wharf.

BOWLES/HOPKINS GALLERY: 47 Beach St, tel 885 4550. Exhibition of prints and graphics.

CORY GALLERIES: 377 Geary St, tel 397 0966 and 360 Jefferson St, tel 771 3664. Good range of 19th-century paintings, plus sculpture and prints.

FREMONT CENTRAL PARK: 40220 Paseo Padre Parkway in Fremont. Large park including a library, lake and waterfowl refuge. Bike and jogging trails. Swimming during the summer months.

GOLDEN GATE BRIDGE: the link between San Francisco and Marin County. 1.7-mile single-span suspension bridge.

GOLDEN GATE PARK: bounded by Lincoln Way, Stanyan and Fulton Sts. 1,017-acre park first developed in 1887 from a sandy wasteland. The park was the brainchild of John McLaren and features many hundreds of plants, trees and shrubs. Also within the grounds are two lakes, a buffalo paddock and a children's playground.

GRACE CATHEDRAL: Nob Hill. Major episcopal church built in 1863. Replicas of Ghiberti's bronze doors in Florence are on the east façade.

LAKESIDE PARK: north shore of Lake Merritt, Oakland. Various attractions including Children's Fairyland (with clown and puppet shows), a garden centre featuring dahlias and chrysanthemums, and a natural science centre containing a wild duck sanctuary.

LATHROP HOUSE: 627 Hamilton Av, tel 366 1350. An example of early Gothic Revival architecture, furnished in period (1860s).

MARINE WORLD/AFRICA USA: $\frac{1}{2}$ mile E off Ralston Av in Redwood City. Combines an oceanarium with African game

collection. Wild animals roam at will behind natural barriers. Water entertainments include trained whales and a reef aquarium.

PACIFIC FILM ARCHIVE: 2621 Durant Av, Berkeley. A large collection of films. Daily showings.

SAN FRANCISCO ZOOLOGICAL GARDENS: Zoo Av, off Sloat Blvd, tel 661 4844. There are over 1,000 creatures in the 70-acre Fleishacker Zoo. Among the more interesting are snow-leopards, pigmy hippos, monkeys and white rhinos. A children's section contains tame animals and amusements. Also within the gardens are a deer park and nature trail.

SKYLINE BOULEVARD: in Oakland. Road following the rim of the city's hills. Fine views of the East Bay.

STANFORD LINEAR ACCELERATION CENTER: Stanford University in Palo Alto. A two-mile-long electron accelerator used to study atomic particles. It is the world's largest scientific instrument.

UNIVERSITY OF CALIFORNIA: E of Oxford St, Berkeley, tel 486 5611. Lovely 720-acre campus. Two-hour guided tours of the Lawrence-Berkeley Laboratory, reservations necessary.

THEATRES

AMERICAN CONSERVATORY THEATER: company at Geary Theater, 415 Geary St, tel 673 6440. Renowned repertory company plus regular guest appearances. Main season runs from October to May.

CANNERY THEATER: The Cannery, 2801 Leavenworth St, tel 441 6800. Variety of theatrical productions.

GOLDEN GATE THEATER: Golden Gate and Taylor Sts, tel 673 4400. A provincial platform for Broadway productions.

MARINES MEMORIAL THEATER: 609 Sutter St. Specialised productions. A sister theatre to the Geary Theater.

THE ORPHEUM: 1192 Market St, tel 552 4002. Mainly stages Broadway spectaculars.

MUSIC

MIDSUMMER MUSIC FESTIVAL: Sloat Blvd and 19th Av. Symphonies, jazz, opera, musicals and ethnic dance groups. Summer months only.

SAN FRANCISCO BALLET: War Memorial Opera House, Van Ness Av, tel 431 1210. Spring and summer seasons.

SAN FRANCISCO SYMPHONY ORCHESTRA: Louise M Davies Symphony Hall, Van Ness Av, tel 431 5400. Season runs from September to May. Pop concerts during the summer.

NIGHTLIFE

San Francisco comes to life when the sun goes down. The best nightclubs are to be found on Broadway, the main street of North Beach. Some of the better known clubs are: Bocce Ball, featuring opera singers; Red Garter, where sing-songs, piano and piano-playing are the order of the day; Finocchio's, where drag artists are featured. Exotic dancers can be found at The Peppermint Tree, The Chichi and The Gigi. Sinaloa, at 1416 Powell St, is the place for Latin entertainment. If you fancy some off-beat cellar entertainment, try The Purple Onion at 140 Columbus Av.

CLIMATE

The temperature in San Francisco rarely falls below 40° Fahrenheit or rises above 70° Fahrenheit. It is unusual to have more than a few hot days in summer, so pack a warm coat. Most of the rain falls in the winter months, but fog appears in the mornings and evenings during the summer. The warmest months are September and October; January is usually the coldest.